Praise for the Weird & Wacky Holiday Marketing Guide

I0105444

"Ginger has created a clever and fascinating resource for you to stand out from the rest. If you are looking to truly make a positive impression, use this book now!"—**Peggy McColl,** New York Times Best-Selling Author

"I absolutely love this! Creating a marketing plan takes work, and this calendar makes it so much easier. This is a 'MUST-HAVE' tool for every author and entrepreneur!" —**Ellen Violette,** Award-Winning Publishing & Platform Building Coach, 6 Time #1 Best-Selling Author & Grammy-nominated Songwriter, www.theebookcoach.com

*"People love to buy. They especially love to buy when they have a reason. The **Holiday Marketing Guide** provides clever marketing strategies to increase sales every month of the year based on events and holidays. It's a brilliant guide for the savvy marketer."* —**Daniel Hall,** Creator of *Free Marketing Tutorials* at DanielHallPresents.com/getcode

"Ginger Marks has put together a fantastic resource! If you are looking for outside of the box ideas for marketing as well as for celebrating, you are going to love the 2016 Weird & Wacky Holiday Marketing Guide. As a former elementary school teacher I wish I had had a copy of this incredible resource when I was teaching. The month-long and week-long holidays, listed throughout this guide, could create the foundation for exciting study units." —**D'vorah Lansky, M.Ed.** Best-Selling author of *Book Marketing Made Easy,* www.BookMarketingMadeEasy.com

"Another awesome read from Ginger packed with quick grab and go marketing ideas to expand your space in this world. Let's face it, in order to capture attention, there has to be a creative hook what better way to align your marketing than with holiday's that offer a creative roll out. The

ideas and positioning for each month are fun and creative with a unique flare. Highly recommend this book for those who are looking for the creative edge in 2016." —**Lauren E Miller,** Google's #1 Stress Relief Expert/International Best-Selling Author/Speaker/Trainer/Coach, www. LaurenEMiller.com

2016 Weird & Wacky 8th Edition
HOLIDAY MARKETING GUIDE

Your business marketing calendar of ideas

Ginger Marks

DocUmeant *Publishing*

244 5th Avenue
Suite G-200
NY, NY 10001
646-233-4366
www.DocUmeantPublishing.com

Volume 8 First Edition, December 2015

Published by DocUmeant Publishing
244 5th Ave, Ste G–200
NY, NY 10001

646-233-4366

Editor Wendy VanHatten
VanHatten Writing Services

www.wendyvanhatten.com

Layout & Design Ginger Marks
DocUmeant Designs

www.DocUmeantDesigns.com

Library of Congress Control Number: 2015918417

ISBN13: 978-1-937801-59-5
ISBN10: 1-937801-59-4

Contents

Foreword

By now you are probably familiar with this unique marketing book. In its eighth edition this ebook offers more new, fun, and easy marketing ideas exclusively penned for the calendar year 2016. Now you can grow your business with strategies built around wacky holidays, observed throughout the world, for the entire 2016 calendar year. If you missed the premier 2009 issue or want to complete your collection, all previous and unique yearly editions are available at http://www.HolidayMarketingGuide.com.

Events are one of the smartest prescriptions for slumping sales and for maintaining a healthy business. It's not enough anymore to merely have goods on the shelf and open the doors on time every day. We all need to reinvent our businesses to keep them thriving and healthy. And, that is just what this ebook intends to help you achieve.

To take advantage of the information provided, pick a date and discover the unusual holidays celebrated on that date. Then, read the corresponding month's "Holiday Marketing Ideas" section to find a simple implementation or allow it to open your creative mind and think of some of your own.

Please note that the asterisk (*) in front of a holiday means a specific holiday is celebrated on that numerical date each year. For example, Christmas Day is December 25 no matter what day that falls on during the calendar week.

Here's another exceptional marketing idea for you I discovered when visiting BrownieLocks.com, and which is now listed in the *Chase Calendar of Events* that I cull from, while preparing the very first edition. Bonza Bottler Days™—the day is the same as the month it is in. That equates to: 1/1, 2/2, 3/3, etc. There is one in every month. There you have it; another extra fine excuse for an event to boost your notoriety and sales each and every month!

This is by no means a comprehensive edition. I have made all attempts to ensure the accuracy of the contents. If you encounter errors, or know of a holiday that needs to be included, please let me know so they can be addressed in future editions.

Read on, have fun, initiate your own version of these holidays, and reap the benefit for your business.

Ginger Marks

P.S. New in this edition I have included a 'Notes to Self' at the close of this book to assist in implementing your Weird & Wacky Holiday Marketing Plan events for 2016.

Annual Dates of Note

International Year of Pulses

The IYP 2016 aims to heighten public awareness of the nutritional benefits of pulses as part of sustainable food production aimed towards food security and nutrition. The Year will create a unique opportunity to encourage connections throughout the food chain that would better utilize pulse-based proteins, further global production of pulses, better utilize crop rotations, and address the challenges in the trade of pulses.

Pulses are annual leguminous crops used for both food and feed. Pulse crops such as lentils, beans, peas, and chickpeas are a critical part of the general food basket. Pulses are a vital source of plant-based proteins and amino acids for people around the globe and should be eaten as part of a healthy diet to address obesity, as well as to prevent and help manage chronic diseases such as diabetes, coronary conditions, and cancer; they are also an important source of plant-based protein for animals.

For more information http://www.fao.org/pulses-2016/en/.

International Year of Camelids

For centuries they have hauled loads up the Andes and through trackless deserts with no more acknowledgment than a slap on the rump. It will "raise awareness at all levels to promote the protection of camelids and the consumption of the goods produced from these mammals in a sustainable manner". For more information visit http://www.un.org/en/ga/search/view_doc.asp?symbol=A/C.2/69/L.41.

Chinese Year of the Monkey[1]

The monkey is a clever animal. It is usually compared to a smart person. During the Spring and Autumn Period (770–476 BC), the dignified Chinese official title of marquis was pronounced 'Hou', the same as the pronunciation of 'monkey' in Chinese. The animal was thereby bestowed with auspicious meaning.

This year, people born in the Year of the Monkey are lucky in almost every aspect of life, except health. Besides their brilliant talents and assiduous efforts, the lucky stars also promote big developments in their career. Abundant wealth will be accumulated due to their economic lifestyle. Meanwhile, they will gain sweet love relationship and stable marriage life in the whole year. However, they need to pay attention to their health condition.

---

1   Travel China Guide. http://www.travelchinaguide.com/intro/social_customs/zodiac/monkey.htm.

Strengths

The general images of people in this zodiac sign are always smart, clever, and intelligent, especially in their career and wealth. They are lively, flexible, quick-witted, and versatile. In addition, their gentleness and honesty bring them everlasting love life. Although they are born with enviable skills, they still have several shortcomings, such as impetuous temper. Besides, they tend to look down upon others. Strengths: enthusiastic, self-assured, sociable, innovative.

Weaknesses

Jealous, suspicious, cunning, selfish, arrogant

JANUARY

MONTH-LONG HOLIDAYS

Jan 6–Feb 9 Carnival Season

Jan 7–Feb 9 Germany: Munich Fasching Carnival

Be Kind to Food Servers Month, Book Blitz Month, Celebration of Life Month, Get a Life Balance Month, Get Organized Month, International Brain Teaser Month, International Child-Centered Divorce Awareness Month, International Creativity Month, International New Year's Resolutions Month for Businesses, International Wayfinding Month, National Be On-Purpose® Month, National Clean Up Your Computer Month, National Glaucoma Awareness Month, National Hot Tea Month, National Mentoring Month, National Personal Self-Defense Awareness Month, National Poverty in America Awareness Month, National Radon Action Month, National Skating Month, National Slavery and Human Trafficking Prevention Month, National Stalking Awareness Month, National Volunteer Blood Donor Month, Oatmeal Month, Shape Up US Month, Teen Driving Awareness Month, Worldwide Rising Star Month

WEEK-LONG HOLIDAYS

Jan 1–3 Japanese Era New Year

Jan 1–7 Diet Resolution Week

Jan 1–8 New Year's Resolution Week

Jan 2–8 Someday We'll Laugh about This Week

Jan 3–9 Home Office Safety and Security Week

Jan 7–10 Elvis Presley Birthday Celebration

Jan 8–10 Vegaspex

Jan 11-17 Cuckoo Dancing Week

Jan 15–17 Art Deco Weekend

Jan 16–17 Bald Eagle Appreciation Day

Jan 17–23 International Handwriting Analysis Week

Jan 18–22 Healthy Weight Week, Sugar Awareness Week

Jan 18–25 Week of Christian Unity

Jan 23–24 Ice Fest

Jan 24–30 Clean Out Your Inbox Week, National Certified Registered Nurse Anesthetists (CRNA) Week

Jan 25–30 National Cowboy Poetry Gathering

Jan 31–Feb 6 Catholic Schools Week, Children's Authors and Illustrators Week

DAILY HOLIDAYS

1. *Bonza Bottler Day™, Canada: Polar Bear Swim, *Copyright Revision Law Signed (1976), *Ellis Island Opened Anniversary (1892), *Emancipation Proclamation (1863), *Euro Introduced (1999), *First Baby Boomer Born–Kathleen Casey Wilkens in Philadelphia, PA (1946), *Haiti: Independence Day, *Mummer's Parade, *New Year's Day, *New Year's Dishonor List Day, St Basil's Day, *Z–Day, *National Environmental Policy Act (1970), Cuba: Liberation Day & Anniversary of the Revolution, Czech–Slovak Divorce (1993; Anniversary of separation into two nations), Stock Exchange Holiday

2. 55 MPH Speed Limit Day (1974), Earth at Perihelion, Haiti: Ancestor's Day, *Happy Mew Year for Cats Day, Japan: Kakizome, Switzerland: Berchtoldstag

3. *Alaska Admission Day, *Drinking Straw Day (1888), Memento Mori Day, Queen for a Day, *Queen for a Day Day, St Geneviève Day

4. *Amnesty for Polygamists: Anniversary (1893), *Dimpled Chad Day, *Elizabeth Ann Bayley–Seton Day, *Pop Music Chart Day, *Trivia Day, *World Braille Day, World's Tallest Building Day

5. *Alvin Ailey (1931), *Five-dollar-a-Day Minimum Wage Day (1914), Twelfth Night

6. *Armenian Christmas, *Epiphany or Twelfth Day, Italy: La Befana, Pan Am Circles Earth, *Three Kings Day

7. *First Balloon Fight Across English Channel (1785), *Harlem Globetrotter's Day, *International Programmers' Day, Japan: Nanakusa, Orthodox Christmas, Trans-Atlantic Phoning (1927)

8. Argyle Day, *Elvis Presley Birth (1935), *Midwife's Day or Women's Day, *National Joygerm Day, *Show and Tell Day at Work, *War on Poverty Day (1964)

9. *Aviation In America Day (1793), *Panama's Martyr Day

10. *National Cut Your Energy Costs Day, Stephen Foster Day, Switzerland: Meitlinsunntig, *United Nations Day

11. *Cigarettes Are Hazardous to Your Health Day, Japan: Coming of Age Day, National Clean Off Your Desk Day, Plough Monday

12. *Haiti Earthquake Day (2010), Poetry at Work Day, *Women Denied Vote (1915)

13. *Radio Broadcasting Day, Sweden: St Knut's Day

14. *Benedict Arnold Day, *Caesarean Section Day, *Ratification Day

15. Arbor Day (Florida), Molière Day, International Fetish Day, Super Bowl Day, Quarterly Estimated Federal Income Tax Payers' Due Date (also Apr 15, Jun 15 and Sep 15, 2015)

16. *Appreciate a Dragon Day, *Civil Service Day, Eagle Days, Japan: Haru-No-Yabuiri, *National Nothing Day, *Religious Freedom Day

17. *Al Capone Day, *Cable Car Day, *Ben Franklin Birthday (1706), *Judgment Day, Kid Inventors' Day, St Anthony's Day, Southern California Earthquake Day

18. *Louis and Clark Expedition Commissioned (1803), Martin Luther King Birthday Observed, National Crowd Feed Day, *Winnie The Pooh Day

19. *Confederate Heroes Day (Texas), *Tin Can Day

20. Brazil: San Sebastian's Day, Rid the World of Fad Diets and Gimmicks Day

21. Get to Know Your Customers Day (third Thursday of each quarter is set aside to get to know your customers even better), First Concorde Flight, *National Hugging Day, Women's Healthy Weight Day

22. *Answer Your Cat's Questions Day, *Celebration of Life Day, *Roe vs. Wade Day, *St Vincent Feast Day

23. Children's Gasparilla Extravaganza and Pirate Fest (Tampa, Florida), Local Quilt Shop Day, *National Handwriting Day, National Pie Day, *Snowplow Mailbox Hockey Day

24. *Belly Laugh Day, *Beer Can Day, *National Compliment Day

25. *A Room of One's Own Day, Bubble Wrap Appreciation Day, First Scheduled Transcontinental Flight, *Macintosh Computer Day (1984), St Dwynwen Day

26. Australia: Cockroach Race Day, Dental Drill Day, India: Republic Day

27. Germany: Day of Remembrance for Victims of Nazism, National Geographic Society Day, *Thomas Crapper Day, United Nations: International Day of Commemoration in Memory of the Victims of the Holocaust, *Viet Nam Peace Day

28. *Challenger Space Shuttle Explosion (1986), Data Privacy Day

29. Canada: Winterlude, Curmudgeons Day, Fun at Work Day, National Preschool Fitness Day, *Seeing Eye Dog Day, *Thomas Paine Day

30. *Inane Answering Message Day, National Seed Swap Day

31. *Inspire Your Heart with Art Day, World Leprosy Day

HOLIDAY MARKETING IDEAS FOR JANUARY

International Wayfinding Month—If I was to tell you that this month-long holiday is about turnstiles you might snicker. Albeit as it may, it's not just in celebration of turnstiles but everything that helps us find our way around and through life. So, as you ponder different ways to use this weird holiday this month why not consider finding ways to help others. Perhaps become a mentor or host webinars or seminars. A very simple action you could take is to send out thank you cards to those who have helped you on your way. How about a coupon for your loyal customers for a discount on your products or services that is only good for the month?

Jan 4 World Braille Day—Today is the day that celebrates Louis Braille and commemorates his life and work; a revolutionary, simple, and effective system for communicating. Since today is all about communication, what better way to celebrate than to keep the lines of communication open any which way you can imagine? In this line of thinking what about sending out tips for communicating with others to your social media contacts? A twitter tips day would be a very easy way to initiate this. Or, you might consider a postcard reminder of the holiday sent out to your customers or handed out to those you come in contact with today. Look for a sample you can modify to your liking in the appendix of this guide.

Courtesy of "Louis Braille by Étienne Leroux" by Agence Rol - Bibliothèque nationale de France. Licensed under Public Domain via Commons

Here's just one more idea. Hold a fundraiser for a school for the blind in your area or donate some braille books to their library. If you do hold a fundraiser don't forget to make the media aware of your plan. A sample press release is always available in the appendix in every Weird & Wacky Holiday Marketing Guide since the very first one.

Jan 8 Argyle Day—Try coercing everyone in your office or family and friends to sport their favorite argyle sweater,

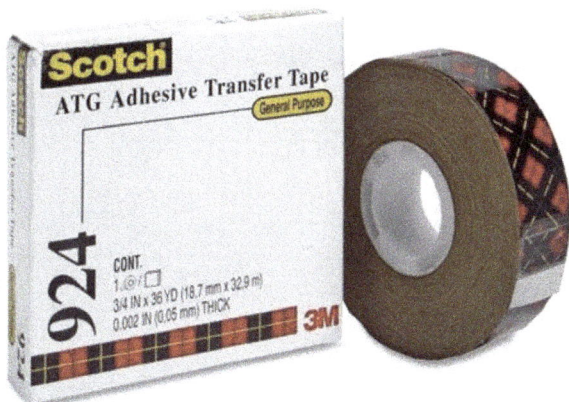

bowtie, or socks and then pose for a photo. Then have an on-line or off-line photo contest. The winner, of course, receives a package of Scotch Brand Argyle tape or, pick up an argyle business card holder from Made by Meg Too! You'll find her link in the Resources appendix.

Jan 16 National Nothing Day—It's back! Our all-time favorite holiday. I couldn't pass up the opportunity to reiterate this favorite from the very first edition of the Weird & Wacky Holiday Marketing Guide. Back then it wasn't a National holiday, so perhaps you'll let me get away with repeating a holiday idea this time. Here's a craft idea that you can sell as a fundraiser or just for the heck of it. Make A Jar of Nothing! You'll find the directions in the appendix.

Jan 21 Women's Healthy Weight Day—The obvious way to celebrate this day is when you work in a fitness or health related world. Do you want to know what these healthy weight levels are? Look in the appendix to find a chart and sample flyer you can use to your advantage.

But, let's look at this on a little different level. Healthy weight might be your capabilities rather than physical presence. Looking at it in this whole new light paves the way for marketing on this Weird & Wacky Holiday for a myriad of other occupations. Coaches, for example, or perhaps those of you who are image consultants may find this the perfect opportunity to market your businesses as well.

If you aren't in one of these fields and can't come up with a twist of your own, then I suggest you partner with other business owners and hold a seminar or webinar on weighing in on the prospects of owning and running a lucrative business.

FEBRUARY

MONTH-LONG HOLIDAYS

Feb 10–Mar 26 Lent

AMD/Low Vision Awareness Month, American Heart Month, Bake for Family Fun Month, Beat the Heat Month, Fabulous Florida Strawberry Month, Festival of the North Month, International Boost Self-Esteem Month, Library Lovers Month, Marfan Syndrome Awareness Month, National African American History Month, National Bird-Feeding Month, National Black History Month, National Cherry Month, National Condom Month, National Mend A Broken Heart Month, National Parent Leadership Month, National Pet Dental Health Month, National Teen Dating Violence Awareness and Prevention Month, National Time Management Month, Plant the Seeds of Greatness Month, Return Shopping Carts to the Supermarket Month, Spay/Neuter Awareness Month, Spunky Old Broads Month, Wise Health Care Consumer Month, Worldwide Renaissance of the Heart Month, Youth Leadership Month

WEEK-LONG HOLIDAYS

Feb 1–5 International Networking Week

Feb 1–7 African Heritage and Health Week, Solo Diners Eat Out Week

Feb 2–8 Publicity for Profit Week

Feb 7–9 Shrovetide

Feb 7–13 Dump Your Significant Jerk Week, Freelance Writers Appreciation Week, Jell-O® Week

Feb 8–9 Fasching

Feb 8–14 Love Makes the World Go Round; but, Laughter Keeps Us from Getting Dizzy Week

Feb 9–11 World AG Expo

Feb 12–15 Great Backyard Bird Count

Feb 14–20 International Flirting Week, Love a Mensch Week, Random Acts of Kindness Week

Feb 14–21 (NCCDP) Alzheimer's & Dementia Staff Education Week

Feb 21–27 Build a Better Trade Show Image Week, National Eating Disorders Awareness Week, National Engineers Week

Feb 26–27 Texas Cowboy Poetry Gathering Days

Feb 28–Mar 5 Telecommuter Appreciation Week

DAILY HOLIDAYS

1. Decorate with Candy Day, Freedom Day, *Robinson Crusoe Day

2. African–American Coaches Day, *Bonza Bottler Day™, *Candelmas, *Groundhog Day, *Hedgehog Day, *Imbolic Sled Dog Day, Mexico: Dia de la Candelaria

3. *Four Chaplains Memorial Day, *Income Tax Birthday, Japan: Bean Throwing Festival Day (Setsubun), National Girls and Women in Sports Day, *The Day The Music Died Day (1959)

4. *Facebook Launch Day (2004), Medjool Date Day, *Rosa Parks Birthday (1913), *USO Day, World Cancer Day

5. American Dental Association Give Kids a Smile Day®, Bubble Gum Day, National Wear Red Day, *Family Leave Bill (1993), Longest War in History Ends (1985), Move Hollywood & Broadway to Lebanon, *Weatherperson's Day, Working Naked Day

6. New Zealand: Waitangi Day, Take Your Child to the Library Day, United Nations: International Day of Zero Tolerance for Female Genital Mutilation

7. *Ballet Day, *Chaplin's "Tramp" Day (1914), *Charles Dickens (1812), Germany: Fasching Sunday, Man Day, Switzerland: Homstrom, *Wave All Your Fingers At Your Neighbor's Day

8. *Boy Scout Day (1910), Chinese New Year, Iceland: Bun Day, Japan: Ha-Ri-Ku-Yo (Needle Mass), Opera Debut in the Colonies Day (1735), Shrove Monday

9. *Ernest Tubb (1914), *Gypsy Rose Lee (1914), Iceland: Bursting Day, International Pancake Day, Mardi Gras, New Mexico: Extraterrestrial Culture Day, Paczki Day, Read in the Bathtub Day, Shrove Tuesday, Union Officers Escape Libby Prison (1864)

10. *"All the News that's Fit to Print" Day, Ash Wednesday, *Charles Lamb (1775), *First Computer Chess Victory Over Human (1996), *Plimsoll Day

11. *First Woman Episcopal Bishop (1989), Get Out Your Guitar Day, *Japan: National Foundation Day, *National Shut-in Visitation Day, *Pro Sports Wives Day, *Satisfied Staying Single Day, *Thomas Alva Edison Birthday (1847), *White Shirt Day

12. *Darwin Day, *Dracula Day, *Abraham Lincoln (1809), NAACP Day, *Oglethorpe Day, *Safetypup's® Day

13. *Employee Legal Awareness Day, *First Magazine Published (1741), *Get a Different Name Day, *Madly In Love With Me Day, World Radio Day, World Whale Day

14. ENIAC Computer Day, *Ferris Wheel Day, *First Presidential Photograph Day (1849), Random Acts of Kindness Day, *League of Women Voters Day, National Donor Day, *National Have-a-Heart Day, Race Relations Day, *St Valentine's Day

15. Asteroid Near Miss Day, Canada: Family Day & Maple Leaf Flag Day, *Galileo, Galilei (1564), *Lupercalia, Presidents' Day, *Remember the Maine Day, *Susan B. Anthony Day, George Washington's Birthday (Observed)

16. Lithuania: Independence Day

17. *League of United Latin American Citizens (LULAC) Founded (1929), *My Way Day, *National PTA Founders Day

18. *Cow Milked while Flying in an Airplane Day, Helen Gurley Brown Day, *Pluto (Planet) Day

19. *Japanese Internment Day

20. *Northern Hemisphere Hoodie Hoo Day (At high noon everyone yells "HoodiE-Hoo" to chase away winter and make way for spring.), *United Nations: World Day for Social Justice

21. Daytona 500, *United Nations: International Mother Language Day

22. Montgomery Boycott Arrests Day (1956), *George Washington (1732), *Woolworth's Day (First Chain store opened 1879)

23. *Curling is Cool Day, Diesel Engine Day, *Iwo Jima Day (flag raised), Single Tasking Day, World Spay Day

24. Gregorian Calendar Day (1582), Inconvenience Yourself™ Day, Mexico: Flag Day, Steve Jobs Birthday (1955), *Wilhelm Carl Grimm (1786)

25. *Jim Backus Birthday (1913), Introduce A Girl to Engineering Day, National Chili Day

26. *Federal Communications Commission Created (1934), *For Pete's Sake Day, *Levi Strauss Day

27. *Henry Wadsworth Longfellow Birthday (1807), Open That Bottle Night, World Sword Swallowers Day

28. Floral Design Day, *National Tooth Fairy Day

29. Bachelors Day, International Underlings Day, Leap Year Day

HOLIDAY MARKETING IDEAS FOR FEBRUARY

Spunky Old Broads Month—How in the world have I missed this one all these years? This February get out there and kick up your heels! Show these young upstarts how we do things. Tweets and FaceBook aren't just for the under 30 crowd. Start a group or share your wisdom in tweets or events.

If you're not a spunky old broad you could rely on Madge's wisdom. Her timeless cartoons will leave your clients and customers laughing and, since you shared it with them you'll bring your name back into their minds more than just when they read your offering, whether it's shared on-line or in the form of a card or note.

Feb 4 Medjool Date Day—Get out your healthy snacks and celebrate this Weird & Wacky Holiday. Any business that has to do with health and wellness should not have a problem coming up with simple marketing plans to promote their business on this healthy holiday.

If you or your business doesn't fit neatly into this category, one really good idea is to schedule the Blood Mobile to visit your business or partner with your city chamber and hold a Blood Drive. You might even sponsor free blood pressure checks at a local grocery store or other business. Then let the press know what you are up to for added punch.

To learn more blood donation opportunities, visit www.givelife.org or call 1-800-GIVE-LIFE (1-800-448-3543).

Feb 6 Take Your Child to the Library Day—If you remember when you first fell in love with the library then you will understand how important libraries are and what a joy they can still prove to be. Why not celebrate this holiday by having a book reading festival? Participate as an author or gather a group of authors and sponsor a special event. With a little forethought and planning the library will assist in the promotion and so will the media. You will find a sample promotional flyer in the appendix waiting for you to customize and make your own.

Feb 7 Man Day—So, we celebrated with Spunky Old Broads Month I guess we have to give our men at least one day. For this one we need to think of things that make our men's hearts go pitter-patter. Tools and gadgets will get most of their hearts throbbing. If you have an intellectual, then books or artifacts may be the way to go. What about golf? I hear a lot of deals are made on the golf course. So how do you meld these into one vast celebration? Rent the local golf club's meeting room and showcase businesses that offer these services and wares.

How about hosting a Man Day contest? Have their family and friends submit the man in their life and tell you in a brief paragraph or two why they think their recommendation deserves the crown of Man of the Day. Then have unbiased judges determine the winner. You might even have a runner up and be sure to let the media know.

Feb 17 National PTA Founders Day—This day is set aside as a reminder of the substantial role that the PTA has played locally, regionally, and nationally in supporting parent involvement and working on behalf of all children and families. It honors the PTA's founders Phoebe Apperson Hearst and Alice McLellan Birney, and the founder of Georgia's Congress of Colored Parents and Teachers, Selena Sloan Butler. Now how's that for getting the scoop on this important day?

Tweet away today and be sure to use the hashtag #PTAExcellence. Offer up your thanks and advice. Find ways to give back to your educational institutions. Things like book drives, special educational opportunities, or donating school supplies to classrooms in your area are just the beginning. As always, get your community involved and let the media know what you are up to, to ensure success.

Feb 29 Leap Year Day—This one takes a little thought. But since it only comes around every four years we definitely need to put our marketing hats on and promote, promote, promote. Don't leave all the fun to your mega stores and malls; dive in and have Leap Year Day Sale or party. If it is too cool in your area of the country host an indoor event. Maybe even a show at a large venue with booth rentals if you are up to the task.

As I understand it, this is the year that women may propose marriage to the men in their lives. I guess this might be a stretch for some of us, but for those who are single and looking, this might be your year!

MARCH

MONTH-LONG HOLIDAYS

Mar 5–20 Iditarod Trail Sled Dog Race

Mar 13–Apr 15 Deaf History Month

Mar 13–26 Passiontide

Alport Syndrome Awareness Month, American Red Cross Month, Colorectal Cancer Awareness Month, Credit Education Month, Employee Spirit Month, Humorists Are Artists Month, International Ideas Month, International Listening Awareness Month, International Mirth Month, Irish-American Heritage Month, Mad for Plaid Month, National Clean Up Your IRS Act Month, National Colorectal Cancer Awareness Month (Different sponsor from Colorectal Cancer Awareness Month), National Craft Month, National Eye Donor Month, National Kidney Month, National Multiple Sclerosis Education and Awareness Month, National Nutrition Month®, National Peanut Month, National Umbrella Month, National Women's History Month, Optimism Month, Play the Recorder Month, Poison Prevention Awareness Month, Red Cross Month, Save Your Vision Month, Sing with Your Child Month, Social Work Month, Women's History Month, Workplace Eye Wellness Month, Youth Art Month

WEEK-LONG HOLIDAYS

Mar 1–7 National Cheerleading Week, National Procrastination Week, Will Eisner Week

Mar 1–14 Japan: Omizutori (Water-Drawing Festival)

Mar 6–12 Celebrate Your Name Week, National Consumer Protection Week, Read an e-Book Week, Return the Borrowed Books Week, Teen Tech Week

Mar 7–11 National School Breakfast Week

Mar 13–19 Camp Fire Birthday Week, Consider Christianity Week, Passion Week, Termite Awareness Week

Mar 14–20 Brain Awareness Week

Mar 14–20 United Kingdom: Shakespeare Week

Mar 18–20 Sherlock Holmes Weekend

Mar 19–20 Military Through the Ages

Mar 20–26 Act Happy Week, Holy Week, International Phace Syndrome Awareness Week, National Animal Poison Prevention Week, National Poison Prevention Week, World Folk Tales & Fables Week

Mar 21–27 United Nations: Week of Solidarity with the Peoples Struggling Against Racism and Racial Discrimination, Wellderly Week

Mar 27–Apr 2 National Protocol Officers' Week, Root Canal Awareness Week

Mar 28–Apr 3 Mule Days

DAILY HOLIDAYS

1. *Iceland: Beer Day, Korea: Samiljol or Independence Movement Day, National Black Women in Jazz and the Arts Day, National Horse Protection Day, *National Pig Day, Paraguay: National Heroes' Day, *Peace Corps Day, Plan a Solo Vacation Day, *Refired, Not Retired Day, Switzerland: Chalandrea Maraz, Town Meeting Day, Wales: St David's Day, World Compliment Day, Zero Discrimination Day

2. Ethiopia: Adwa Day, *Dr Seuss Day, *Highway Numbers Day, *King Kong Premier (1933), NEA's Read Across America Day

3. *Bonza Bottler Day™, International Ear Care Day, Japan: Hina Matsuri (Doll Festival), *National Anthem Day (1931), Simplify Your Life Day, United Kingdom & Ireland: World Book Day, United Nations: World Wildlife Day, *What If Cats and Dogs Had Opposable Thumbs Day

4. *Courageous Follower Day, Dress in Blue Day, National Day of Unplugging, *National Grammar Day, Old Inauguration Day, World Day of Prayer

5. St Piran's Day

6. *Dred Scott Day, *Michelangelo (1475), Namesake Day

7. Australia: Eight Hour Day or Labor Day, Fun Facts About Names Day, National Be Heard Day, Suez Canal Day

8. International Working Women's Day, National Proofreading Day, Organize Your Home Office Day, Unique Names Day, United Nations: Day for Women's Rights & International Peace, United States Income Tax Day (1913)

9. *Barbie Day, Discover What Your Name Means Day, Panic Day, Registered Dietitian Nutritionists Day

10. International Bagpipe Day, *Mario Day, Nametag Day, *Salvation Army Day, *Telephone Invention Day, *US Paper Money Day, World Kidney Day

11. Dream 2016 Day, *Johnny Appleseed Day, Middle Name Pride Day

12. Blame Someone Else Day, *FDR's First Fireside Chat (1933), Genealogy Day, *Girl Scout Day, International Fanny Pack Day, Moshoeshoe's Day

13. Check Your Batteries Day, Daylight Savings Time Begins, *Earmuffs Day, Good Samaritan Involvement Day, IUGR Awareness Day, National Open an Umbrella Indoors Day, Passiontide, Smart and Sexy Day

14. *Albert Einstein Birthday (1879), Fill Our Staplers Day (also Nov 7), Moth-er Day, Orthodox Green Monday, Pi Day (as in the math pie = 3.14159265 etc.)

15. Brutus Day, Ides of March, True Confessions Day

16. *Black Press Day (1827), Curlew Day, Freedom of Information Day, *Goddard Day, *Lips Appreciation Day, No Selfies Day

17. Absolutely Incredible Kid Day, *Campfire USA Day, Ireland: National Day, St Patrick's Day

18. *Electric Razor Day, Forgive Mom and Dad Day, *National Biodiesel Day

19. Earth Hour, Wyatt Earp (1848), National Quilting Day, *Operation Iraqi Freedom Day (2003), St Joseph's Day, Save the Florida Panther Day, Swallows Return to San Juan Capistrano Day, US Standard Time Act (1918)

20. *Great American Meat Out Day, Japan: Vernal Equinox Day, Kiss Your Fiancé Day, Ostara, Palm Sunday, *Proposal Day®, *United Nations: International Day of Happiness, *Won't You Be My Neighbor Day

21. *First Round-the-World Balloon Flight (1999), India: New Year's Day, Memory Day, National Renewable Energy Day, *Twitter Day, *United Nations: International Day for the Elimination of Racial Discrimination, United Nations: Poetry Day, United Nations: International Day of Forests, World Down Syndrome Day

22. American Diabetes Association Alert Day, As Young As You Feel Day, *Equal Rights Day, *International Day of The Seal, *Louis L'Amour Day (1908), Laser Patented Day (1960), *National Goof-off Day, *World Day for Water (aka World Water Day)

23. Beat the Clock Day, "Big Bertha Paris Gun Day, *Liberty Day, National Puppy Day, National Tamale Day, *Near Miss Day, "OK" Day, *United Nations: World Meteorological Day

24. Maundy Thursday or Holy Thursday, Purim, United Nations: International Day for the Right to the Truth Concerning Gross Human Rights Violations and for the Dignity of Victims, *World Tuberculosis Day

25. *Bed In for Peace Day, Feast of the Annunciation, Good Friday, *Greece: Greek Independence Day: National Day of Celebration of Greek & American Democracy, *Houdini Day (1874), Maryland Day, National Medal of Honor Day, *Old New Year's Day, Pecan Day, Tolkien Reading Day, United Nations: International Day of Remembrance of The Victims of Slavery and The Transatlantic, United Nations: International Day of Solidarity with Detained and Missing Staff Members

26. *Legal Assistants Day, *Make Up Your Own Holiday Day

27. Easter Even, Easter Sunday, European Union: Daylight Savings Time (Summertime begins), *FDA Approves Viagra Day, *Quirky Country Music Song Titles Day

28. Mule Day, Seward's Day, South Africa: Family Day, Switzerland: Egg Races

29. *Knights of Columbus Founders Day, *National Mom & Pop Business Owner's Day, *Niagara Falls Runs Dry (1848), *Texas Loves The Children Day

30. Anesthetic Day, *Doctors Day, Grass is Always Browner on the Other Side of the Fence Day, *Pencil Day, World Bipolar Day

31. *Bunsen Burner Day, Cesar Chavez Day, *Eiffel Tower Day (1998), International Hug a Medievalist Day, *National "She's Funny That Way" Day

HOLIDAY MARKETING IDEAS FOR MARCH

Mar 28–Apr 3 Mule Days—Mules are the workhorse for humans. That being the case, your event with a mule as a theme speaks to the basics. As you plan your event think about what you can share that will help others by sharing basic how to's. Check out the Mule Days Poster in the appendix that I have designed for you as well as the donkey silhouette that I have created. Feel free to use on postcards, posters, websites, and all your marketing pieces to promote your event.

Mar 4 Courageous Follower Day—Every good leader needs actively engaged followers. So, today is the perfect time to thank those courageous followers and loyal customers. Send out emails, postcards, or notes of thanks for their continued support. Perhaps you could host a very in-depth training just for them or a super sale that only they are invited to participate in.

Mar 10 Telephone Invention Day—Oh my goodness! How would we ever survive without the invention of the telephone? After all, the telephone used to be our main means of communication. This leads me to think about marketing ideas for this Weird & Wacky Holiday in two ways. First, and most obviously, would be to host tele-seminars. The second is marketing around training on how to properly communicate. Perhaps you are educating others on how to handle difficult customers, or maybe speaker training. What about communicating how to live a healthier lifestyle? Now, open your mind and start thinking about how you can communicate with your specific audience.

Mar 20 Won't You Be My Neighbor Day—In celebration of Mr. Rogers of Mr. Roger's Neighborhood fame who taught us that respecting those around us and having a good attitude is just as important as learning the basics taught in school. So, to highlight this Weird & Wacky Holiday, throw your marketing hat into the ring and don your 70s sweater and go out and do something, anything, neighborly. Take a group of singers to a nursing home and sing some 70s tunes to the residents. Or, bake some goodies and have a bake sale and donate the money from the sales to your local SPCA.

Want to hear his famous tune? Visit the link below or click the image (https://vimeo.com/122032164).

Mar 24 Houdini Day—Here's another great man, Harry Houdini, lecturer, athlete, author, expert on the history of magic, exposer of fraudulent mediums, and motion picture actor. Best known for escaping restraints such as handcuffs, straightjackets, coffins, boxes and, yes Virginia, milk cans.

To celebrate this holiday gear your marketing to thoughts about how to escape. Travel agents, you know what to do. But, for the rest of us it is more a matter of teaching by hosting seminars, webinars, or teleseminars on these subjects.

As Houdini was a remarkable athlete, if your business is health related you too have a good reason to market your success. As Karen Mullarkey, Personal Trainer, says, "No Excuses, and that's No Mullarkey!"

Mar 27 Quirky Country Music Song Titles Day—This is your chance to have a ton of fun! Gather a group, have a contest, and see who can come up with the most unique and funny title for a hot new country music song. No fair using the one listed by Thomas & Ruth Roy of WellcatHolidays in Chase Calendar of Events, "Put Me Out at the Curb Darlin', 'Cause the Recycling Truck's A-Comin', and You Done Thrown me Out" (©2006 by WH).

APRIL

MONTH-LONG HOLIDAYS

Alcohol Awareness Month, Community Spirit Days Month, Couple Appreciation Month, Defeat Diabetes Month, Distracted Driving Awareness Month, Grange Month, Holy Humor Month, Home Improvement Time Month, Informed Women Month, International Customer Loyalty Month, International Twit Award Month, Jazz Appreciation Month, Library Snapshot Days, Mathematics Awareness Month, Month of the Young Child®, National African-American Women's Fitness Month, National Autism Awareness Month, National Cancer Control Month, National Card and Letter Writing Month, National Child Abuse Prevention Month, National Decorating Month, National Donate Life Month, National Exchange Club Child Ab use Prevention Month, National Humor Month, National Knuckles Down Month, National Occupational Therapy Month, National Pecan Month, National Pest Management Month, National Poetry Month, National Rebuilding Month, National Sexual Assault Awareness Month, Nationally Sexually Transmitted Diseases (STDs) Month, National Soy Foods Month, National Youth Sports Safety Month, Pet First Aid Awareness Month, Pharmacists War on Diabetes Month, Prevention of Animal Cruelty Month, Rosacea Awareness Month, School Library Month, Straw Hat Month, Stress Awareness Month, Women's Eye Health & Safety Month, Workplace Conflict Awareness Month, Worldwide Bereaved Spouses Awareness Month

WEEK-LONG HOLIDAYS

Apr 1–7 APAWS International Pooper-scooper Week, Laugh at Work Week, Testicular Cancer Awareness Week (aka Get A Grip Day)

Apr 2–3 Just Pray No! Worldwide Weekend of Prayer and Fasting

Apr 3–9 National Week of the Ocean, National Window Safety Week

Apr 4–10 Explore Your Career Options Week, Hate Week–"Down with Big Brother"

Apr 10–16 National Library Week, National Volunteer Week, Pan–American Week, Week of the Young Child

Apr 11–15 Undergraduate Research Week

Apr 12–14 England: London Book Fair

Apr 15–17 Global Youth Service Day

Apr 16–24 National Park Week

Apr 17–23 Greece: Dumb Week, National Coin Week, National Karaoke Week

Apr 18–24 Cleaning for a Reason Week

Apr 21–24 Fiddler's Frolics

Apr 23–30 Historic Garden Week in Virginia, Money Smart Week®

Apr 24–30 Administrative Professionals Week, National Scoop the Poop Week, Orthodox Holy Week, Sky Awareness Week, World Immunization Week

Apr 25–29 Fibroid Awareness Week, National Playground Safety Week

Apr 26–May 2 Preservation Week

Apr 29–May 1 National Dream Hotline® Days

Apr 29–May 5 Japan: Golden Week Days

DAILY HOLIDAYS

1. *April Fools or All Fools Day, Mylesday, *National Fun at Work Day, Pascua Florida Day (Observed), Reading is Funny Day, *Sorry Charlie Day

2. *Sir Alec Guinness (1914), *International Children's Book Day, International Pillow Fight Day, National Ferret Day, National Love Your Children Day, National Love Your Produce Manager Day, Ponce de Leon Discovers Florida (1513), *Reconciliation Day, *United Nations: World Autism Awareness Day

3. Blacks Ruled Eligible to Vote Day (1944), *Pony Express Day, National Weed Out Hate: Sow the Seeds of Peace Day, *Tweed Day

4. *Beatles Take Over Music Charts (50th Anniversary), *Bonza Bottler Day™, Taiwan: Children's Day, *United Nations: International Day for Mine Awareness & Assistance in Mine Action, *Vitamin C Day

5. *Helen Keller's Miracle Day, National Deep Dish Pizza Day, National Equal Pay Day

6. Drowsy Driver Awareness Day, Paraprofessional Appreciation Day, *Tartan Day, *Teflon Day (1938), Thailand: Chakri Day, United Nations: International Day of Sport for Development and Peace, Whole Grain Sampling Day

7. *International Beaver Day, International Snailpapers Day, *Metric System Day, National Alcohol Screening Day, National Beer Day (1933), *No Housework Day, United Nations: International Day of the Reflection on the Genocide in Rwanda, *United Nations: World Health Day

8. Home Run Record Set by Hank Aaron (1974), International Roma Day, Japan: Flower Festival (Hana Matsuri), National Dog Fighting Awareness Day, Poll Tax Outlawed Day

9. *Civil Rights Bill of 1866 Day, Civil War Ends (1865), *Jenkins Ear Day, Jumbo the Elephant Day, National Former Prisoner of War Recognition Day, *Winston Churchill Day

10. *Commodore Perry Day, *National Siblings Day, *Safety Pin Day, *Salvation Army Founder's Day

11. *Barbershop Quartet Day, *International "Louie Louie" Day

12. Children's Day in Florida (always the second Tuesday), National Be Kind to Lawyers Day, *National D.E.A.R. Day (aka Drop Everything and Read), *National Licorice Day, Polio Vaccine Day, United Nations: International Day of Human Space Flight, *Walk on Your Wild Side Day

13. *Guy Fawkes Day, India: Vaisakhi, National Bookmobile Day, *Thomas Jefferson Day

14. Celebrate Teen Literature Day, *Children with Alopecia Day, Dictionary Day (1828), *International Moment of Laughter Day, National Library Workers Day, Pan American Day, Pan–American Day in Florida, Pathologists' Assistant Day, Spring Astronomy Day

15. Boston Marathon Bombing (2013), Botox Day, *McDonald's Day, *Deaf School Day, *Income Tax Pay Day, *National Take a Wild Guess Day, *National That Sucks Day, Quarterly Estimated Federal Income Tax Payers' Due Date (also Jan 15, Jun 15, and Sep 15, 2015), *Titanic Sinking (1912)

16. *Charlie Chaplin Day (1889), National Auctioneers Day, Record Store Day, *Natural Bridges National Monument Day, Save the Elephant Day

17. *Blah! Blah! Blah! Day, *Ellis Island Family History Day, National Haiku Poetry Day

18. Boston Marathon (120th Running), The House that Ruth Built Day, *International Amateur Radio Day, Stress Awareness Day, Paul Revere's Ride Day (1775), *Pet Owners Independence Day, Zimbabwe: Independence Day

19. Branch Davidian Fire at Waco (1993), Education and Sharing Day (tentative), John Parker Day, National Hanging Out Day, Oklahoma City Bombing (1995), Patriots Day in Florida

20. International Cli-Fi Day

21. Aggie Muster Day, Brazil: Tiradentes Day, Get to Know Your Customers Day (third Thursday of each quarter is set aside to get to know your customers even better), Indonesia: Kartini Day, *Kindergarten Day, National Bulldogs are Beautiful Day, National High Five Day, Red Baron Shot Down Day, San Jacinto Day

22. Coins Stamped "In God We Trust" Day, *Chemists Celebrate the Earth Day, *Earth Day, *Movie Theatre Day, *National Jelly Bean Day, Oklahoma Land Rush Day (1889), United Nations: International Mother Earth Day

23. Lazarus Saturday, National Dance Day, Pesach or Passover *Public School Day, St George Feast Day, Spain: Book Day and Lover's Day, United Nations: English Language Day, *United Nations: World Book & Copyright Day, William Shakespeare Day (1564), World Book Night

24. Ireland: Easter Rising (1916), Library of Congress Day, Mother-Father Deaf Day, Orthodox Palm Sunday, Switzerland: Landsgemeinde

25. Anzac Day, Egypt: Sinai Day, *License Plates Day, World Malaria Day, World Penguin Day

26. *Confederate Memorial Day, *Hug An Australian Day, National Help a Horse Day, National Pretzel Day, *Richter Scale Day, United Nations: World Intellectual Property Day

27. Administrative Professionals Day or Secretary's Day, *Babe Ruth Day (1947), Mantanzas Mule Day, *Morse Code Day, Most Tornadoes in a Day (US), National Little Pampered Dog Day

28. Biological Clock Gene Discovered (1994), Canada: National Day of Mourning, Easter Monday, Take Our Daughters and Sons to Work® Day (fourth Thursday in April), United Nations: World Day for Safety and Health at Work, Workers Memorial Day

29. Japan: Showa Day, National Arbor Day, National Hairball Awareness Day, National Teach Children to Save Day, *Peace' Rose Day, United Nations: Day of Remembrance for all Victims of Chemical Warfare, Zipper Day (1913)

30. Beltane, *Bugs Bunny Day (1938), Día de los Niños/Día de los Libros, International Jazz Day, National Animal Advocacy Day, National Honesty Day (Honest Abe Awards), National Rebuilding Day, *Spank Out Day USA, *Walpurgis Night, World Healing Day, World Tai Chi and Qigong Day, World Veterinary Day

HOLIDAY MARKETING IDEAS FOR APRIL

Stress Awareness Month—For the entire month of April the theme is Stress Awareness. We need to think about ways to de-stress in business and our personal lives. If you sell beauty related products, sexy lingerie, candles, or bath products this month-long holiday is custom made for you. Are you into skin care? Dermatologists and authors who write about them would ingratiate today's youth by giving them advice on fighting acne and other skin related problems. Even diet and others in health related fields, including mental health professionals, should tap into this marketing opportunity.

Now, another thing that can totally stress us out is job loss and financial lack. So career professionals, personal presence experts, speaking coaches, as well as financial advisors, will benefit from focusing their marketing in this direction. Flyers, brochures, seminars, school presentations, and samples are all good ways to get the word out this month.

Apr 24–30 Sky Awareness Week—Celebrate the beauty of nature this week. Events can be held at schools, nature centers, and Agricultural Extension Services in your local area. Walks for a cause might be a good idea. Share your event with your local media and watch them turn out and spread the news.

How about having a photo contest? This is really easy to do and can be accomplished both on and off-line. Since this is a celebration of weather and astronomy don't just limit the photo subject to clouds. Focus on interesting day and/or night sky photos.

Apr 8 International Roma Day—In Europe the Roma culture is a segment of people who have been discriminated against for centuries; much like others here in the USA. To show your support for solidarity of those repressed races among us those who teach tolerance need to stand up and be heard. Lift your heads high and let the biased around you know, 'We're not going to take it anymore!'

Events that would easily bring peoples of all walks of life as well as cultures would be International Food Fairs that focus on Ethnic Customs and dress. Participate, for sure; sponsor, definitely! And don't forget to send out your press release and post flyers to let everyone know about your event well in advance.

Apr 14 International Moment of Laughter Day—This Weird & Wacky Holiday is sure to make even the most stoic among us smile. Whether you snort, guffaw, or roll on the floor in a belly laugh it matters not. Just don't roll your eyes and look away. Join in the fun, celebrate by sharing funny stories and jokes, or even have a Laugh-a-Thon for a good cause. You don't have to charge a huge fee to attendees, simple donations can add up quickly when you share your event on-line in social media circles. After all, we all know laughter is good medicine.

Apr 15 National That Sucks Day—Is it just me or is it a coincidence that National That Sucks Day is celebrated on the day the IRS sucks us dry with taxes!? If that's not enough to get your dander up, I don't know what will. A sure fire way to market your business today would be to hand out suckers with your business card or a ribbon label with your business name on it. If you can find custom wrappers that have National That Sucks Day emblazoned on them so much the better! If you want to double wrap them with a custom wrapper use the template in the appendix and add a quote on the inside like they do with certain chocolates.

Also, you might be interested to know that in the *2011 Weird & Wacky Holiday Marketing Guide* you will find in the appendix a list of common candy wrapper sizes, a bar wrapper template, and some mini wrapper designs.

Apr 23 United Nations: English Language Day—Do you share the love of the English language? Whether you write and speak American, Canadian, European, or even with a southern drawl, English is the language of the world and today is our day to celebrate that fact. So, today share your love of the English language by sharing with English as a second language folks who will be grateful for your help.

This can be done both on-line and in person. Grammar girls unite, editors hold fast, writers write your hearts out. Make every word count. Poetry contests, writing contests, word puzzles, and many more ideas are waiting for you to take advantage of the wonderful world of English. Be sure to look in the appendix for some simple word games to get you on your way.

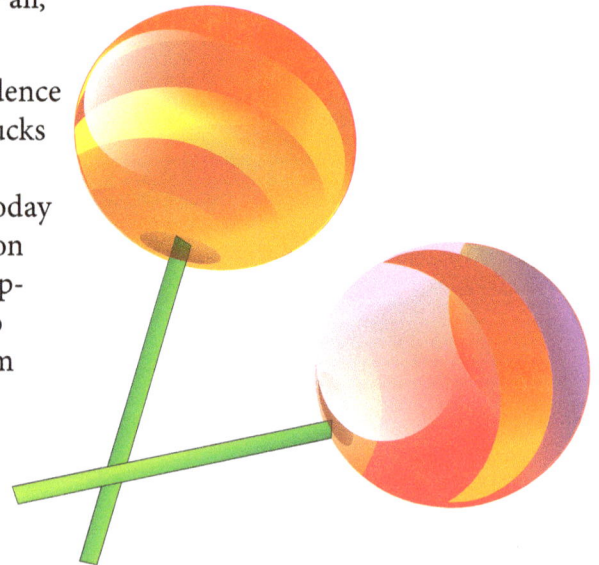

MAY

MONTH-LONG HOLIDAYS

May 29–Jun 4 Black Single Parent's Week

Asian/Pacific American Heritage Month, Asthma Awareness Month, Better Hearing and Speech Month, Fibromyalgia Education and Awareness Month, Gardening for Wildlife Month, Get Caught Reading Month, Gifts from the Garden Month, Global Civility Awareness Month, Haitian Heritage Month, Heal the Children Month, Healthy Vision Month, Home Schooling Awareness Month, Huntington's Disease Awareness Month, International Mediterranean Diet Month, International Victorious Woman Month, Jewish American Heritage Month, Law Enforcement Appreciation Month (Florida), Melanoma/Skin Cancer Detection and Prevention Month, Motorcycle Safety Month, Mystery Month, National Allergy/Asthma Awareness Month, National Arthritis Awareness Month, National Barbecue Month, National Bike Month, National Foster Care Month, National Good Car-Keeping Month, National Hamburger Month, National Hepatitis Awareness Month, National Meditation Month, National Mental Health Month, National Military Appreciation Month, National Osteoporosis Awareness and Prevention Month, National Photo Month, National Physical Fitness and Sports Month, National Preservation Month, National Salad Month, National Stroke Awareness Month, National Sweet Vidalia® Onion Month, National Vinegar Month, Older American's Month, React Month, React Month, Spiritual Literacy Month, Strike Out Strokes Month, Ultraviolet Awareness Month, Women's Health Care Month, Young Achievers/Leaders of Tomorrow Month

WEEK-LONG HOLIDAYS

May 1–7 Be Kind to Animals Week®, Choose Privacy Week, Goodwill Industries Week, National Family Week, National Pet Week

May 2–3 and May 2–6 National Library Legislative Day and Virtual Library Legislative Day

May 2–6 PTA Teacher Appreciation Week

May 2–8 Children's Book Week, National Wildflower Week, Work at Home Moms Week

May 6–12 National Nurses Week

May 8–14 National Hug Holiday Week, National Nursing Home Week, Salute to 35+ Moms Week

May 9–13 National Etiquette Week

May 9–15 National Stuttering Awareness Week, Spring Astronomy Week

May 15–21 International New Friends Old Friends Week, National Police Week, National Transportation Week, Police Week, World Trade Week

May 21–22 Fishing Has No Boundaries Days

May 21–27 National Safe Boating Week

May 22–28 National Hurricane Preparedness Week

May 23–30 National Backyard Games Week

May 25–31 Fleet Week New York 2016, United Nations: Week of Solidarity with the Peoples of Non-self-governing Territories

DAILY HOLIDAYS

1. *Amtrack, *Executive Coaching Day, *Keep Kids Alive—Drive 25® Day, Labor Day, *Law Day, *Lei Day, *Loyalty Day, *May Day, Mother Goose Day, Motorcycle Mass and Blessing of the Bikes, National Bubba Day, National Infertility Survival® Day, *New Home Owners Day, Orthodox Easter Sunday or Pascha, Rogation Sunday, Rural Life Sunday or Soil Stewardship Sunday, Russia: International Labor Day, *School Principals' Day

2. King James Bible Day, Labor Day (Observed), Melanoma Monday

3. *Garden Meditation Day, James Brown (1993), Japan: Constitution Memorial Day, *Lumpy Rug Day, Mexico: Day of the Holy Cross, National Public Radio Day, National Specially-Abled Pets Day, National Teachers Day, *National Two Different Colored Shoes Day, *United Nations: World Press Freedom Day, World Asthma Day

4. China: Youth Day, Great American Grump Out, *International Respect for Chickens Day, Japan: Greenery Day, *Star Wars Day

5. AMA Founded Day (1847), Ascension Day, *Bonza Bottler Day™, *Cartoonists Day, *Cinco de Mayo, International Day of the Midwife, Japan: Children's Day, Martin Z Mollusk Day, National Day of Prayer, National Day of Reason

6. Babe Ruth's First Major League Home Run (1915), Hug Your Cat Day, *Joseph Brackett Day, Military Spouse Appreciation Day, *No Diet Day, *No Homework Day, Orson Wells Day (1915)

7. Beaufort Scale Day, Free Comic Book Day, Join Hands Day, Kentucky Derby, Mother Ocean Day, National Babysitters Day, National Cosmopolitan Day

8. Mother's Day, Mother's Day at the Wall, *No Socks Day, *United Nations: Time of Remembrance & Reconciliation WWII (8–9), *V E Day, *World Red Cross Red Crescent Day

9. National Moscato Day, Russia: Victory Day

10. Golden Spike Driving Day, *World Lupus Day

11. Book Expo America Trad Exhibit (11-13, Chicago), *Eat What You Want Day, Donate A Day's Wages To Charity Day, National Nightshift/Thirdshift Workers Day, National Receptionists Day, National School Nurse Day

12. *Limerick Day, *Odometer Day

13. Blame Someone Else Day, Fintastic Friday: Giving Sharks a Voice Day, Friday the Thirteenth, National Hummus Day

14. Bookcon 2016, International Migratory Bird Celebration (Day), Jamestown Day, Letter Carriers "Stamp Out Hunger" Food Drive, *Jamestown Day, *Lewis and Clark Expedition Sets Out Day (1804), *Small Pox Vaccine Discovered (1796), Spring Astronomy Day, Stay Up All Night Night, *The Stars and Stripes Forever Day, *Underground America Day, WAAC Day (1942), United Nations: World Migratory Bird Day, World Fair Trade Day

15. Flight Attendant Day, Hyperemesis Gravidarum Awareness Day, Japan: Aoi Matsuri (Hollyhock Festival), Mexico: San Isidro Day, National Sliders Day, *Nylon Stockings Day, *Peace Officer Memorial Day, Pentecost, WhitSunday, *United Nations: International Day of Families

16. *Academy Awards Day (1929), *Biographer's Day, *First Woman to Climb Mt Everest Day (1975), Mimosa Day, WhitMonday

17. *First Kentucky Derby Day (1875), *Same-Sex Marriages Day (2004), Germany: Waldchestag (Forest Day), *United Nations: World Telecommunications and Information Society Day

18. Haiti: Flag and University Day, *International Museum Day, *Visit Your Relatives Day

19. *Boys Club Day, National Hepatitis Testing Day, National Scooter Day

20. *Amelia Earhart Atlantic Crossing Day (1932), *Eliza Doolittle Day, International Virtual Assistants Day, Lindbergh Flight (1927), Mecklenburg Day, National Bike to Work Day, *National Defense Transportation Day, *National Pizza Party Day, Teacher's Day in Florida, *Weights & Measures Day

21. *American Red Cross Founder's Day, Armed Forces Day, *I Need A Patch For That Day, National Learn to Swim Day, *National Wait Staff Day, *United Nations: World Day for Cultural Diversity for Dialogue & Development

22. *Canadian Immigrants' Day, *National Maritime Day, Neighbor Day, Strongest Earthquake in the 20th Century (1960), Trinity Sunday, *United Nations: International Day for Biological Diversity, US Colored Troops Founders Day, World Goth Day

23. *Bonnie and Clyde Death (1934), Canada: Victoria Day, *Declaration of the Bab Day, *International World Turtle Day®, United Nations: International day to End Obstetric Fistula

24. *Brother's Day, International Tiara Day, *Morse Code Day

25. African Freedom Day, *Ralph Waldo Emerson (1803), *Jessie Owens' Day, *National Missing Children's Day, National Senior Health and Fitness Day, *National Tap Dance Day, Poetry Day in Florida, *Towel Day, United Nations: Week of Solidarity with Peoples of Non-Self-Governing Territories

26. Australia: Sorry Day, Corpus Christi, National Eat More Fruits and Vegetables Day, John Wayne (1907), World Lindy Hop Day

27. *Cellophane Tape Day, *Golden Gate Bridge Day

28. *Amnesty International Founded (1961), Dionne Quintuplets (1934), Julia Pierpoint Day, *Sierra Club Day, *Slugs Return From Capistrano Day

29. *Amnesty for Southern Rebels Day, *Indianapolis 500 (1911), *Mount Everest Summit Reached (1953), *United Nations: International Day of United Nations Peacekeepers

30. *First American Daily Newspaper Published (1783), *Loomis Day, *Memorial Day (Traditional), Prayer for Peace, Memorial Day, *World Trade Center Recovery and Cleanup Ends (2002)

31. *Copyright Law Passed (1970), *United Nations: World No–Tobacco Day, *What You Think Upon Grows Day, *Walt Whitman Day

HOLIDAY MARKETING IDEAS FOR MAY

May 1 Loyalty Day—It's time for us to turn marketing focus toward our most valued customers and clients. We all know it is less costly to keep a client than to gain a new by seven times. So, take the time to find a special way to show them how important they are to you. If you know them well enough, send them a care package. Do they live for chocolate? What about the dad or mom stressed out by job and family obligations? If you don't know them that well, don't you think it is time you should? If not, a coffee shop gift card is a small token that you can send in a nice Thank You card. If you can though, try to make it something a tad more personal.

Remember, this isn't for ALL your customers and clients, but instead it is for just a very select few. Perhaps those that you haven't heard from in a while would be a good list to focus on.

May 3 Garden Mediation Day—Spiritual leaders take heart. This day is the perfect opportunity for you to focus your marketing around. While today is the day set aside to commune with nature, pulling weeds, planting and pruning, today can also be considered as a time to reflect on the glory of nature itself. Whether you take a group out and hold a 'Garden Retreat', host an on-line event, schedule readings (hopefully of your book), or share poetry your followers and those interested in improving their lives through awareness will join you.

So, if you are in any self-help, fitness, or healing field, consider putting on a *Garden Event* in your local area. Imagine how wonderful it would be to do your morning workout like they do in Japan, together outside, communing with nature!

May 10 Golden Spike Driving Day—This is a the day that the USA was finally connected from coast to coast. As this is a historical day of significance we could begin our marketing efforts with the thoughts of unity. Unity of peoples and unity of country means working together to accomplish much.

So, as you think about ways to market your business today consider events or activities that have a common theme of working together.

One idea that came immediately to mind was getting a group together to help those less fortunate or incapable of helping themselves. Things like painting their homes, as Habitat for Humanity does, or simply shopping for them are easy to accomplish. If you get a good group together find time to write a press release as acts of kindness are often media attractors.

May 16 Biographers Day—Biography: a written account of another person's life. Whether you are writing your own or that of someone else today is the day to pick up your pen and write the history your family will thank you for putting to paper. Writing classes, or story telling days would be good ways to celebrate today. Why not start a biography of your business or an organization? Keep thinking along these lines and you are sure to come up with an inspiration for how to tie your marketing into this Weird & Wacky Holiday.

May 23 International World Turtle Day®—Did you know that there is actually a NY Turtle & Tortoise Society http://nytts.org/nytts/sem2015.htm? For those who live in coastal areas this is a chance to show your community spirit. Join with other business owners and organizations to help protect our turtles. Besides, who can resist spending a day at the beach? Add some fun and hold Human turtle races. You can hand out flyers with your business emblazoned prominently on them or find ways to educate the beach lovers in your community. Be sure to look in the appendix for a sample flyer that you can use and modify.

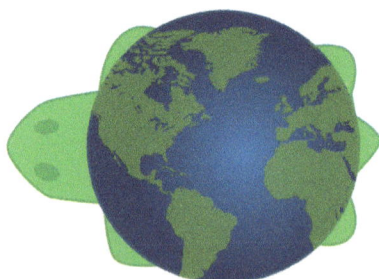

WORLD TURTLE DAY
May 23rd

JUNE

MONTH-LONG HOLIDAYS

Adopt A Shelter Cat Month, African–American Music Appreciation Month, Audiobook Appreciation Month, Cancer From the Sun Month, Caribbean–American Heritage Month, Cataract Awareness Month, Child Vision Awareness Month, Children's Awareness Month, Dairy Alternative Month, Effective Communications Month, Entrepreneurs & Do It Yourself Marketing Month, Fireworks Safety Month, Gay & Lesbian Pride Month, Great Outdoors Month, International Men's Month, International Surf Music Month, June Dairy Month, Perennial Gardening Month, GLBT (Gay, Lesbian, Bisexual & Transgender) Pride Month, Men's Health Education and Awareness Month, Migraine Awareness Month, National Aphasia Awareness Month, National Bathroom Reading Month, National Candy Month, National Caribbean–American Heritage Month, National GLBT Book Month, National Iced Tea Month, National Oceans Month, National Rivers Month, National Rivers Month, Nation Safety Month, National Soul Food Month, National Zoo and Aquarium Month, Pharmacists Declare War on Alcoholism Month, PTSD Awareness Month, Rebuild Your Life Month, Skyscraper Month, Sports America Kids Month, Student Safety Month

WEEK-LONG HOLIDAYS

Jun 4–11 International Clothesline Week

Jun 5–11 Bed Bug Awareness Week, National Business Etiquette Week

Jun 6–12 National Automotive Service Professionals Week

Jun 9–12 Canada: Winnipeg International Children's Festival

Jun 9–16 National Nursing Assistants Week

Jun 12–18 National Flag Week

Jun 13–20 National Hermit Week

Jun 19–25 Carpenter Ant Awareness Week, Lightning Safety Awareness Week

Jun 20–26 Meet a Mate Week, United Kingdom: National Insect Week

Jun 25–26 ARRL Field Day

Jun 26–Jul 2 National Mosquito Control Awareness Week

DAILY HOLIDAYS

1. China: International Children's Day, Gay and Lesbian Pride Day, Kenya: Madaraka Day, National Running Day, Say Something Nice Day, Superman Day, United Nations: Global Day of Parents

2. *Heimlich Maneuver Day, St Erasmus Day, United Kingdom: Coronation Day, *Yell Fudge at the Cobras in North America Day (Don't laugh, I haven't seen any lately!)

3. Bahamas: Labor Day, *Chimborazo Day, Confederate Memorial Day, *First Woman Rabbi (1972), *Mighty Casey Struck Out Day (1888), National Donut Day, Zoot Suit Riots Anniversary (1943)

4. National Trails Day, Pulitzer Prize Day (1917), *United Nations: International Day of Innocent Children Victims of Aggression Day

5. *AIDS First Noted (1981), *Apple II (1977), Children's Awareness Memorial Day, *Hot Air Balloon Day (1783), Japan: Day of the Rice God, National Cancer Survivors Day, *United Nations: World Environment Day

6. *Bonza Bottler Day™, *D–Day (1944), *Drive in Movie Day (1933), National Thank God It's Monday Day, National Yo-yo Day, Prop 13 (1978), *SEC Day (1934), Sweden: National Day

7. *(Daniel) Boone Day, Malta: National Day, *VCR Day

8. National Caribbean-American HIV/AIDS Awareness Day, *United Nations: World Ocean Day, *Upsy Daisy Day, World Oceans Day

9. *Donald Duck Day, International Archives Day, Korea: Tano Day, Orthodox Ascension Day, Toy Industry Association Day

10. *AA Day (1935), *Ball Point Pen Day (1943), American Mint Day (1652), Germany: Bachfest Leipzig, Jordan: Great Arab Revolt and Army Day

11. Belmont Stakes, Jacques Cousteau (1910), *Kamehameha Day (First Hawaiian King), Shavout (begins at sundown)

12. *Baseball's First Perfect Game (1880), Children's Sunday, Multicultural American Child Awareness Day, Loving v Virginia Day (1967), National Jerky Day, Race Unity Day, Russia: Russia Day, *"Tear Down This Wall" Day, United Nations: World Day Against Child Labor

13. Roller Coaster Day (1884), Queen's Official Birthday (Selected Nations)

14. Alzheimer Day, *Family History Day, *Flag Day, Japan: Rice Planting Festival, UNIVAC Computer Day, National Flag Day: Pause for the Pledge, US Army Day, World Blood Donor Day

15. *Magna Carta Day (1215), Native American Citizenship Day, *Nature Photography Day, Quarterly Estimated Federal Income Tax Payers' Due Date (also Jan 15, Apr 15, June 15, and Sep 15, 2015), United Nations: World Elder Abuse Awareness Day

16. *Bloomsday, *Ladies' Day (Baseball), Recess At Work Day

17. *Apartheid Day, Bunker Hill Day, Iceland: Independence Day, *United Nations: World Day To Combat Desertification and Drought, Work@Home Father's Day

18. *Battle of Waterloo (1815), Egypt: Evacuation Day, Longest Dam Race Day, Polar Bear Swim, World Juggling Day

19. Belmont Stakes Day, Family Awareness Day, Father's Day, *Garfield the Cat Day (1978), Husband Caregiver Day, *Juneteenth, Orthodox Pentecost, "War is Hell" Day (1879), *World Sauntering Day

20. Anne and Samantha Day (also Dec 21), *First Doctor of Science Earned by a Woman Day (1895), Midsummer Day, *United Nations: World Refugee Day, *Woman Runs the House Day

21. Go Skateboarding Day, Midsummer Day/Eve Celebrations, World Humanist Day, World Music Day

22. Baby Boomer's Recognition Day, Malta: Mnarja, Stupid Guy Thing Day

23. *Let It Go Day, Runner's Selfie Day, Typewriter Day, United Nations: International Widows Day, United Nations: Public Service Day, Watermelon Thump and Seed-Spitting Contest Day

24. Canada: St John the Baptist Day, *Celebration of the Senses Day, China: Macau Day, Take Your Dog To Work Day®

25. Great American Backyard Campout Day, Supreme Court Ruling Day (Abortion Notification, Bans School Prayer, Upholds Rights to Die), United Nations: Day of the Seafarer

26. America's Kids Day, *Barcode Day, Log Cabin Day, Supreme Court Strikes Down Defense of Marriage Act (2013), *United Nations: International Day Against Drug Abuse and Illicit Trafficking, *United Nations: International Day in Support of Victims of Torture

27. *Decide To Be Married Day, *Happy Birthday to "Happy Birthday To You" Day, Industrial Workers of the World Day, *National HIV Testing Day, PTSD Awareness Day

28. National Columnist's Day

29. Corpus Christi (US Observance), *Death Penalty Ban Day, St Peter and Paul Day, St Peter's Day

30. *Leap Second Adjustment Time Day, National Handshake Day, *NOW (National Organization of Women) Founded Day (1966)

HOLIDAY MARKETING IDEAS FOR JUNE

National Soul Food Month—Calling all hands. Time to hit the kitchen for some downhome comfort food! If you love good home cooked meals like I do you will be delighted to know the whole month of June is National Soul Food Month. Gather your family and friends and enjoy picnicking together or just meet up at Grandma's for a culinary delight.

Things you can do to market your business include recipe swaps, food fairs, cooking classes, and even cookware demonstrations. If you do the latter or even all of these at an event be sure to get the cookware companies to sponsor your event. They may even be willing to send a rep to do the demonstration for you. You can find a flyer in the appendix that will inspire your promotional art.

Jun 8 Upsy Daisy Day—This is a great day to use to market any business! While it is about getting up in a good mood, you can gear your marketing to things that make you feel good. Another way to think about today is that you could have a seminar that helps mentor or train other new business owners. Things you know and have expertise in could very well be just what someone else needs to know. So, schedule a webinar event and share your knowledge with others, or get a group together and make it a full day of sharing.

Jun 12 Multicultural American Child Awareness Day—Does this Weird & Wacky Holiday tug at your heartstrings like it does mine? This is a day that we all should celebrate. It is about sharing the talents and treasures that make up the diversity that is America. Learning about other nationalities and embracing the traditions that make them unique can make a significant dent in fighting prejudice.

In fact, being National Soul Food Month as well as Multicultural American Child Awareness Day, you might consider holding your event today and having speakers as well as food share knowledge and awareness too.

Jun 16 Bloomsday—Today we celebrate Leopold Bloom the central character in James Joyce's *Ulysses*. This is the anniversary of events in Dublin that were recorded in this famous book. Celebrations have been taking place in Ireland and across the globe since at least 1924. It is traditional to dress up as characters from the book or its time frame, visiting each of the locations described in the book (likely in order!). Additionally, there are readings, walks, and discussion of the book and Joyce himself.

So while we look at different ways to focus our marketing efforts today break into an Irish jig and raise your pint up high. It's time to let the Irish in you out for all to see. No need to wait for St Patty's Day! Get your Irish on today and have a perfectly joyous Irish event. And be sure to have a reading of this famous book by someone dressed up in circa 1866 costume.

If you aren't up to having an event then at least send out cards that show your support for the Irish among us. You'll find a sample card in the appendix for use. If you need help getting it customized to fit your business send me a quick email or give me a call and I'll be happy to assist you for a nominal fee.

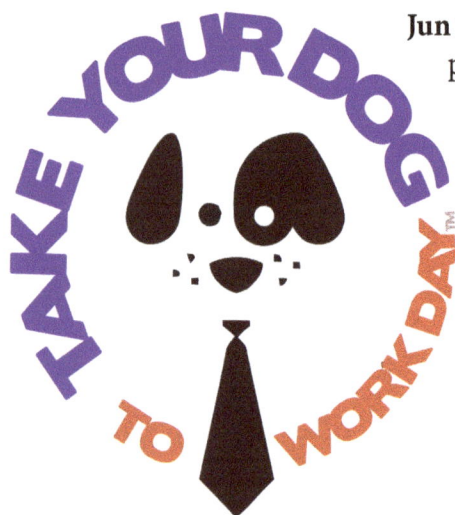

Jun 24 Take Your Dog To Work Day®—Besides a sure-fire way to boost company morale, the national press garnered by Take Your Dog to Work Day is guaranteed to generate lots of good public relations for companies who choose to participate.

Be sure to check out the appendix resources page for more information about this Weird & Wacky Holiday and the Official Take Your Dog to Work Day website, Pet Sitters International. There they have lots of cool ideas. I have pulled their tips on having a successful office event and placed it in the appendix to make it easy for you.

JULY

MONTH-LONG HOLIDAYS

Jul 3–Aug 11 Dog Days

Jul 3–Aug 15 Air Conditioning Appreciation Days

Alopecia Month for Women—International, Bioterrorism/Disaster Education & Awareness Month, Cell Phone Courtesy Month, Herbal/Prescription Awareness Month, International Blondie and Deborah Harry Month, International Zine Month, National "Doghouse Repairs" Month, National Grilling Month, National Horseradish Month, National Hot Dog Month, National Ice Cream Month, National Make a Difference to Children Month, National Minority Mental Health Awareness Month, National Recreation & Parks Month, National Vacation Rental Month, Women's Motorcycle Month, Worldwide Bereaved Parents Awareness Month

WEEK-LONG HOLIDAYS

Jul 1–3 National Tom Sawyer Days

Jul 1–7 National Unassisted Homebirth Week, Old Home Week

Jul 3–9 Be Nice to Jersey Week

Jul 4–10 Nude Recreation Week

Jul 10–16 National Farrier's Week, Sports Cliché Week

Jul 17–23 Captive Nations Week

Jul 7–14 Spain: Running of the Bulls

Jul 18–25 Restless Leg Syndrome (RLS) Education and Awareness Week

Jul 21–24 Comic–Con International, Hemingway Look–alike Contest

Jul 23–31 National Moth Week

Jul 29–31 Annie Oakley Days

Jul 31–Aug 6 Single Working Women's Week

DAILY HOLIDAYS

1. Canada: Canada Day, China: Half-year Day, *Estée Lauder Day (1906), *First Photographs Used in Newspaper Report (1848), *First Scheduled Television Broadcast (1941), First US Postage Stamp Issued (1847), First US Zoo (1874), *IRS Day (1862), Halfway Point of 2016, *Second Half of the New Year Day, *Zip Code Day, Zoo Day

2. *Civil Rights Day, *Constitution Day (USA), Declaration of Independence Resolution (1776), United Nations: International Day of Cooperatives

3. *Canada: Québec Founded, *Compliment Your Mirror Day, Ducktona 500, *Stay Out Of The Sun Day

4. *Anne Landers (95th Anniversary), Caribbean Day or Caricom Day, Celebration of the Cane Day, Declaration of Independence Signing (1776), Earth at Aphelion, *Fourth of July or Independence Day, *Independence-from–Meat Day, *Lou Gehrig Day (1939)

5. *Bikini Day, *National Labor Relations Day

6. Name That Tune Day, *Rabies Inoculation Day, *Take Your Webmaster to Lunch Day

7. *Bonza Bottler Day™, *Father–Daughter Take a Walk Together Day, Japan: Tanabata (Star Festival), *Tell The Truth Day

8. *SCUD Day (Savor the Comic, Unplug the Drama)

9. Bald Is In Day, Carver Day, *Martyrdom of The Bab, Stone House Day

10. *Clerihew Day, *Don't Step On A Bee Day

11. Bowdler's Day, *Day of the Five Billion, International Town Criers Day, *United Nations: World Population Day

12. Family Feud Day (1976), Northern Ireland: Orangemen's Day

13. *Embrace Your Geekness Day, *Gruntled Workers Day, France: Night Watch (Bastille Day)

14. Children's Party at Green Animals Day

15. Japan: Bon Odori (Feast of Lanterns), *Rembrandt Day, *St Swithin's Day

16. Atomic Bomb Test Day, National Woodie Wagon Day, Toss Away the "Could Haves" and "Should Haves" Day

17. Disneyland Opened (1955), National Ice Cream Day, Minimum Legal Drinking Age at 21 Day, Puerto Rico: Muñoz–Rivera Day, "Wrong Way" Corrigan Day (1938)

18. Japan: Marine Day (Third Monday in July), Mandela Day, National Get Out of the Doghouse Day, Red Skelton Day (1913), United Nations: Nelson Mandela International Day

19. *Art Linkletter (1912), Elvis Presley First Single Day

20. Hot Dog Night, Riot Act Day, *Special Olympics Day, Take Your Poet to Work Day

21. Get to Know Your Customers Day (third Thursday of each quarter is set aside to get to know your customers even better), *Hemmingway (1899), *National Women's Hall of Fame Day (1979), No Pet Store Puppies Day

22. *Pied Piper Day, *Rat-catchers Day, *Spooner's (Spoonerism) Day

23. Egypt: Revolution Day, *Hot Enough for Ya Day, Japan: Soma No Umaoi (Wild Horse Chasing), National Day of the Cowboy

24. Auntie's Day, *Cousins Day, Amelia Earhart Day, *National Drive-Thru Day, *National Tell An Old Joke Day, Pioneer Day

25. *Test–Tube Baby Day (1978)

26. Americans with Disabilities Day, Armed Forces Unified (1947), Cuba: National Day (1953), Curaçao Day, *George Bernard Shaw (1856)

27. *Atlantic Telegraph Day, *Insulin Isolated Day (1921), *National Korean War Veterans Armistice Day, *Take Your Houseplant for a Walk Day, *Walk on Stilts Day

28. Beatrix Potter Day, Peru: Independence Day, Singing Telegram Day (1933), World Hepatitis Day, World War I Begins (1914)

29. *NASA (1958), *Rain Day

30. Elvis Presley's First Concert (1954), *Emily Brontë (1818), Henry Ford Day, *Paperback Books (1935), United Nations: International Day of Friendship, United Nations: World Day Against Trafficking in Persons

31. *US Patent Office Opened (1790)

HOLIDAY MARKETING IDEAS FOR JULY

National Make a Difference to Children Month—This month children are out of school and so it is not a surprise to anyone that this Weird & Wacky Holiday is for the whole month of July. Taking it a step further . . .

July 1 Zoo Day—So, I suggest you combine the two and take a group of underprivileged or terminally ill children to the Zoo in your neighborhood. Watching their eyes light up when they see or pet the animals is worth every moment of frustration dealing with the more difficult children. Schools can take advantage of this too and have the summer school children write a report after the fact to keep it educational.

If you play your cards right, so to speak, you may even find a local radio or TV station that will sponsor your event. At the very least let them know what you are up to.

I have even heard that for the month of July some zoos let kids in free when accompanied by adults. So, be sure to call the zoo near you while you are still in the planning stages.

Jul 13 Gruntled Workers Day—How are you doing? Are you happy at work? Are you pleased with your employees? What about your customers and clients, do you have some that hold a special place in your heart and mind? Well today is the day for you to let others know just how wonderful you feel about them and about life.

What you say? 'Gruntled', doesn't that mean upset? Well no, according to Merriam-Webster: Gruntled is *"to put in a good humor."* Thus, on Gruntled Workers Day we celebrate the people who are satisfied in their work and are truly having fun at their jobs.

If you are really feeling bodacious print up a few of the Gruntled Worker stickers in the appendix to hand out today and pick up the spirits of those you come in contact with. Then wish everyone you meet today "Happy Gruntled Workers Day" and when they look at you strange just smile knowingly.

Also in the appendix you will find a workplace poster that you may freely use and share.

Jul 15 Rembrandt Day—Here's another opportunity to double up on the July celebrations. If you are an artist or designer who wants to get known, use your talent to share with others who want to learn your craft. When you gear it around children you'll double up; when you invite adults who are just beginning to work on their craft, such as book cover designers, you can easily see how this would be a wonderful way to let the world or your local populace know you even exist.

Another chance to market your talent is to create an art day festival or show, or perhaps have an awards contest. Since Rembrandt is well-known for his self-portraits be sure to include caricatures and children's art in your contest.

Jul 24 National Drive-Thru Day—Today we celebrate the ease of fast-food dining. Everywhere you look restaurants are making it easy for their customers to pick up a bite without even getting out of their cars. Even elegant dining

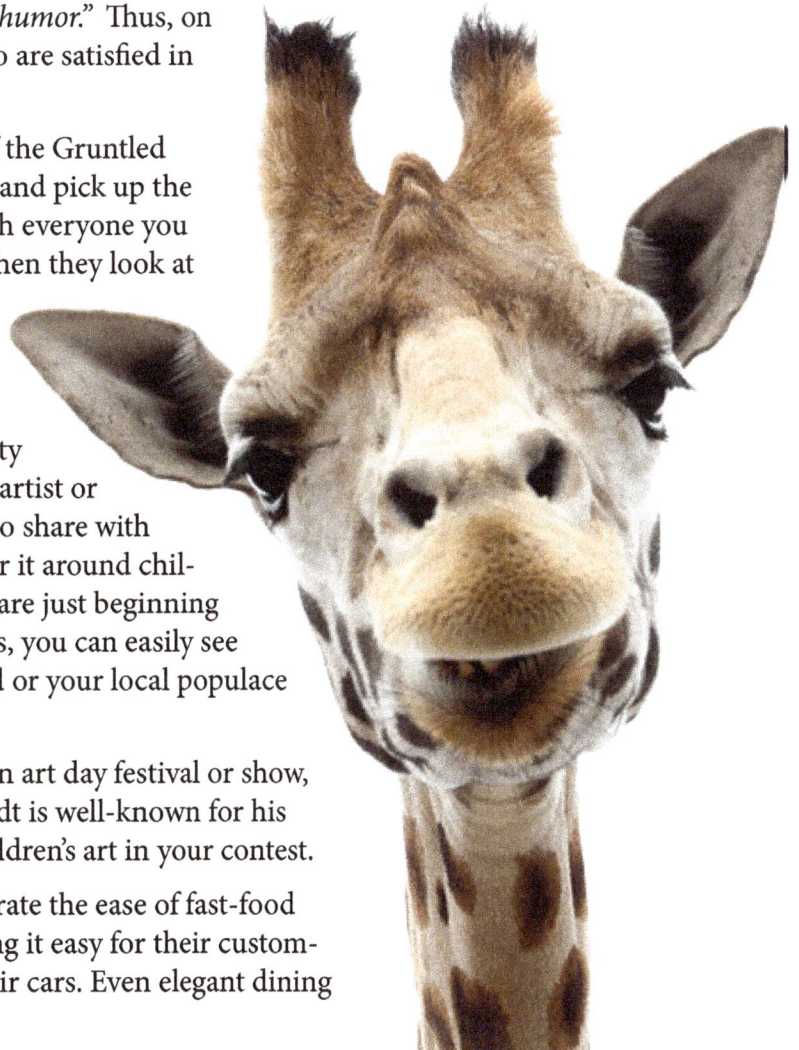

establishments, like Carrabbas, are waking up to the benefit of offering curb-service. If your business isn't looking for how to make your customers lives easier, you too are missing the proverbial boat.

So, today your focus should be on your customers and their convenience. Look for ways to make it easy for them. Whether it is to learn how you can help them save time or money, or sharing your coaching skill, they are sure to notice.

Jul 30 United Nations: International Day of Friendship—What a terrific way to end the month of July as you focus on your clients as friends. Send them a snail mail note or card, or even just a postcard, to let them know how important they are to you and your business. You might even gift them with a box of chocolates or something that they would appreciate. After all, they are your friends as well as clients, and so you should know what they like, right?

This is one sure way to keep your business in their minds and hearts. And we all know how much easier and less costly it is to keep a customer than to find new ones!

Courtesy of http://www.myfbcover.in/typography-facebook-covers/my-friends-rock-facebook-cover.html

AUGUST

MONTH-LONG HOLIDAYS

American Adventures Month, Black Business Month, Boomers Making a Difference Month, Bystander Awareness Month, Children's Eye Health & Safety Month, Children's Vision & Learning Month, Get Ready for Kindergarten Month, National Immunization Awareness Month, National Spinal Muscular Atrophy Awareness Month, National Traffic Awareness Month, Read-A-Romance Month, Shop On-line for Groceries Month, What Will Be Your Legacy Month

WEEK-LONG HOLIDAYS

Aug 1–5 Exhibitor Appreciation Week, Psychic Week

Aug 1–7 International Clown Week (First full week), National Bargain Hunting Week, National Minority Donor Awareness Week, World Breastfeeding Week

Aug 7–9 Hatfield–McCoy Feud Days

Aug 7–13 Assistance Dog Week, National Exercise with Your Child Week, National Health Center Week

Aug 8–12 Weird Contest Week

Aug 9–13 Perseid Meteor Showers

Aug 10–16 Elvis Week

Aug 11–14 National Hobo Days

Aug 12–17 Mae West Birthday Gala

Aug 15–21 National Aviation Week

Aug 25–31 Be Kind to Humankind Week

Aug 29–Sep 5 Burning Man 2015

DAILY HOLIDAYS

1. Australia: Picnic Day, Bahamas: Emancipation Day, Canada: Civic Holiday, Colorado Day, Emancipation of 500 Day, *Girlfriend's Day, *Lughnasadh, *Respect for Parents Day, Rounds Resounding Day, *Spiderman Day, Switzerland: Confederation Day, United Kingdom: Minden Day, *US Census Day, *US Customs Day, Word Lung Cancer Day, *World Wide Web (1990)

2. Costa Rica: Feast of Our Lady of Angels, *Declaration of Independence: Official Signing (1776), National Night Out

3. Columbus Sails for the New World (1492)

4. *Coast Guard Day, Queen Elizabeth, The Queen Mother Birthday, Single Working Woman's Day

5. Braham Pie Day

6. *Hiroshima Day, *Lucille Ball Day (1911), National Mustard Day, Right to Vote Act (1965)

7. Hatfield-McCoy Feud Eruption Day, Herbert Hoover Day (Sunday nearest Aug 10th), *Mata Hari Day (1876), National Lighthouse Day, *Particularly Preposterous Packaging Day, *Professional Speakers Day, Sister's Day®

8. *Bonza Bottler Day™, *Odie Day (1978), *Sneak Some Zucchini Onto Your Neighbor's Porch Night, Victory Day

9. China: Chinese Valentine's Day (aka. Double Seven Day), Japan: Moment of Silence (Bombing of Nagasaki), *Moment of Silence Day, Singapore: National Day, South Africa: National Women's Day, *United Nations: International Day of The World's Indigenous People, *Veep Day

10. Candid Camera Day, National S'mores Day, Nestlé Day (1814), *Smithsonian Day

11. Japan: Yama No Hi (Mountain Day), President's Joke Day (1984), St Clare of Assisi: Feast Day

12. *Home Sewing Machine Day, *IBM PC Day, Night of the Murdered Poets, *United Nations: International Youth Day, *Vinyl Record Day

13. *Alfred Hitchcock (1899), *Annie Oakley Day (1860), Berlin Wall Erected (1961), *International Left Hander's Day, Middle Children's Day, National Garage Sale Day

14. *Navajo Nation: Code Talkers Day, *Social Security Day, Tisha Bav or Fast of Ab Day, *V–J Day (1945)

15. *Assumption of the Virgin Mary, *Best Friends Day, Canada: Yukon Discovery Day, *Chauvin Day, Check the Chip Day, India: Independence Day, Korea: Independence Day, Liechtenstein: National Day, *National Aviation Day, *National Relaxation Day, *Panama Canal Day (1914), Transcontinental US Railway Completion (1870), *Woodstock (1969)

16. *Joe Miller's Joke Day, Klondike Gold Discovery Day, National Roller Coaster Day

17. China: Festival of Hungry Ghosts, *Clinton's "Meaning of 'Is' Is" Day (1998), *Davy Crockett (1786), Gabon: Independence Day, Indonesia: Independence Day, *Mae West (1893)

18. *Bad Poetry Day, *Birth Control Pills Day, *Mail–Order Catalog Day, National Badge Ribbon Day, Serendipity Day

19. Afghanistan: Independence Day, *Black Cow (Root Beer Float) Day, Don Ho Day (1930), United Nations: World Humanitarian Day

20. International Geocaching Day, International Homeless Animals Day® and Candle-light Vigils, *Plutonium Day

21. *American Bar Association Day, *Poet's Day

22. *Be An Angel Day, *International Yacht Race Day, *Southern Hemisphere Hoodie-Hoo Day, Vietnam Conflict Begins (1945)

23. Gene Kelly (1912), *United Nations: Day For The Remembrance of the Slave Trade & Its Abolition, *Valentino Day

24. *Pluto Demoted Day, *Vesuvius Day, William Wilberforce Day

25. Founders Day, India: Krishna Janmashtami, *Kiss–and–Make-Up Day, *National Park Service Day, *Wizard of Oz Day (1939)

26. Baseball Day (First Televised, 1939), *National Dog Day, *Women's Equality Day

27. International Bat Night, *Mother Teresa Day, *The Duchess Who Wasn't Day

28. *March on Washington (1963), *Race Your Mouse Around the Icons Day, *Radio Commercials Day

29. *According to Hoyle Day, Hong Kong: Liberation Day, *More Herbs, Less Salt Day, United Nations: International Day Against Nuclear Tests

30. Huey P Long Day, National Grief Awareness Day, *National Holistic Pet Day, United Nations: International Day of Victims of Enforced Disappearances

31. Kazakhstan: Constitution Day, *Love Litigating Lawyers Day, Malaysia: Freedom Day, Spain: La Tomatina, Trinidad and Tobago: Independence Day

HOLIDAY MARKETING IDEAS FOR AUGUST

Aug 8–12 Weird Contest Week—This week bodes fun for all! How about a pogo stick jumping contest? Jumping for joy could be your theme. Or just the opposite, what about a smooth sailing theme with toy boat races. Of course the content of your event would be speakers who can focus on these themes. In my interview on the *Weird & Wacky Holiday Marketing Guide* website (www.HolidayMarketingGuide.com) I suggested that a mandella coloring book creator host a *Weird Contest* and have the company that their images are designed around become a sponsor. Then create a book with the winning design on the cover.

In the *2010 Weird & Wacky Holiday Marketing Guide* I suggested a Super Hero Impersonation contest, among others. That's a fun contest that is worth repeating, don't you think? What will you do? How will you promote your business this week? Whatever you do, be sure to throw in a healthy dose of fun!

Aug 5 Braham Pie Day—Where would we be without pies? Cakes and cookies are good, but nothing beats a hot piece of pie with a dollop of whipping cream or ice cream. Since pies are on the agenda why not get a group together and make it a truly sensational pie focused event. Take a hint from the "Homemade Pie Capital of Minnesota" and offer up pies, crafts, and contests to make for a 'well-rounded' pie day celebration. (See the resource section for more information.)

If a huge event is not in your future, then perhaps a pie sale or a recipe swap is more to your liking. Either way, on-line or off, these can be accomplished easily. And if you donate to a charity, then you will certainly want to let the media know.

Aug 7 National Lighthouse Day—Do you know what a lighthouse and your business have in common? They are shining beacons to others who need them. So, focus your marketing today on instructing and educating your clients and customers.

Mentors and coaches of all callings, teachers, preachers, and spiritual guides schedule your trainings on-line or live and in living color. When you partner with your local Food Bank you can request attendees to donate to your charity of choice or request a small entry fee with a portion of the proceeds going to the charity. Now you can even hold a Virtual Food Drive. Check the appendix for a flyer example and more information on how to host a Virtual Food Drive. If you want to know how to put on a live Food Drive you'll find that information in the 2014 Weird & Wacky Holiday Marketing Guide starting on pg 118.

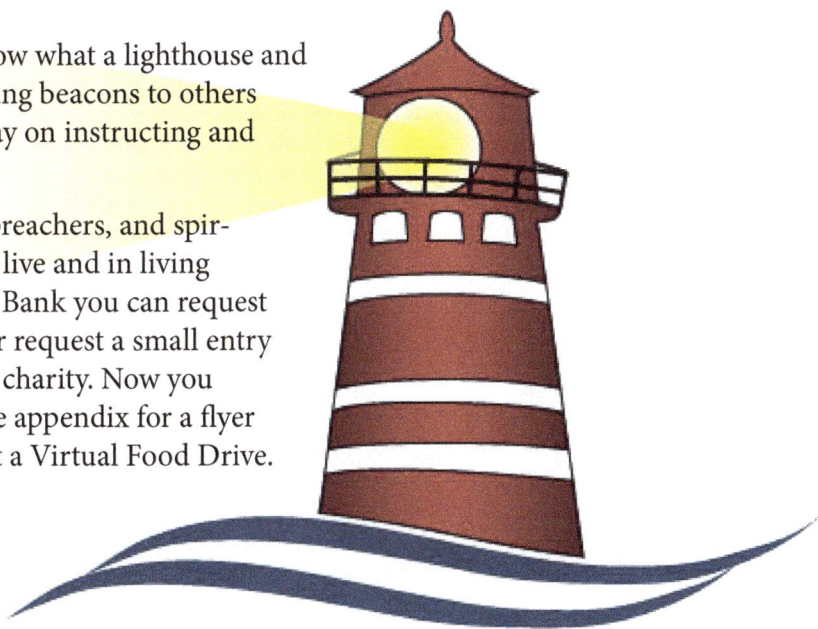

Aug 13 National Garage Sale Day—
Today's Weird & Wacky Holiday gives a clue as to what we should be doing; cleaning out our closets (in more way than one). While you are at it why not think of it as helping others find the treasure that you no longer need? In that vein, other than hosting a clean-out or a garage sale why not consider your knowledge as a thing of worth. Sharing through training, teaching, or coaching or even just speaking at a live or on-line event is an easy way to transfer the 'wealth'.

So, host your National Garage Sale Day event virtually and share with others who are looking for the treasures of knowledge and experience you have accumulated over the years.

Aug 16 Joe Miller's Joke Day—Today is the day to share your wit and spunk. Joe Miller was a famous jokester who made a huge impact on the Brits with his Weird & Wacky sense of humor. So how could we not pick the Weird & Wacky Holiday named after him to focus on this year? You can download a book full of his dry British humour through the link in the Resources.

But, how do you incorporate dry humour into your business marketing? Easy! Have a comedy event or contest. Either can be held on-line or off-line; whatever is your preference.

If you can't abide the English humour then how about just challenging yourself to tell at least one joke today? Jokes can be as simple as one line or as complicated as a whole story. Or what about sharing a few joke facts? If you are as terrible a joke teller as I am you may want to go this route. Also, if you do go this route you might be able to either send an email or postcard with a few pertinent facts about jokes.

One last comment about jokes is in just how healthy laughter is to us. They, whoever they is, say, "Laughter is the best medicine." So be sure to include a bit every day this year. And tell anyone who sneers at your jokes, the doctor told you so.

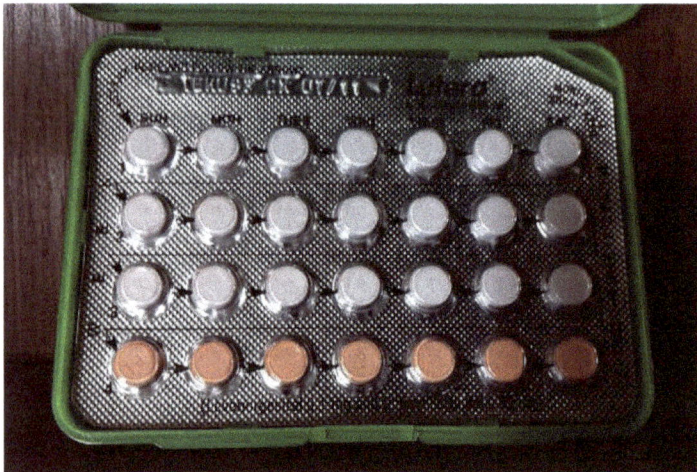

Aug 18 Birth Control Pills Day—Why, or rather How can a business expect to promote their business on this Weird & Wacky holiday? Well, as Homer Simpson would say, "Doah!" What is birth control? It is the assurance of growth in the proper time frame. Therefore, this Weird & Wacky Holiday can be about teaching others that fast and furious is not the way to create long-term growth and success in business.

Now that I have you thinking along those lines, what comes to mind is basic business growth advice. So, pull together those in your industry that can speak on these important topics and host an event that will ensure true success for all attendees. I bet if you go for it you might even get a rep from the Small Business Association to share. What have you got to lose?

SEPTEMBER

MONTH-LONG HOLIDAYS

Sep 7–18 Paralympic Games

Sep 15–Oct 15 National Hispanic Heritage Month

Sep17–Oct 2 Oktoberfest

Sep 26–Oct 1 Banned Books Week—Celebrating the Freedom to Read

AKC Responsible Dog Ownership Month, Atrial Fibrillation Month, Attention Deficit Disorder Month, Be Kind To Editors & Writers Month, Childhood Cancer Awareness Month, Chili: National Month, Fall Hat Month, Great American Low–Cholesterol, Low–fat Pizza Bake Month, Gynecology Cancer Awareness Month, Happy Cat Month, Hunger Action Month, Intergeneration Month, International Speak Out Month, International Women's Friendship Month, Library Card Sign–up Month, National Childhood Obesity Awareness Month, National DNA, Genomics & Stem Cell Education Month, National Head Lice Prevention Month, National Honey Month, National Mushroom Month, National Ovarian Cancer Awareness Month, National Preparedness Month, National Prostate Cancer Awareness Month, National Recovery Month, National Rice Month, National Service Dog Month, National Shake Month, National Skin Care Awareness Month, National Wilderness Month, One-on–One Month, Ovarian Cancer Awareness Month, Pleasure Your Mate Month, September is Healthy Aging® Month, Shameless Promotion Month, Sports Eye Health & Safety Month, Subliminal Communications Month, Update Your Resume Month, Whole Grains Month

WEEK-LONG HOLIDAYS

Sep 1–7 Brazil: Independence Week, Self-University Week

Sep 4–10 National Waffle Week

Sep 5–11 National Stearman Fly-In, National Suicide Prevention Week, Substitute Teacher Appreciation Week

Sep 6–10 Play Days

Sep 11–17 United Kingdom: Battle of Britain Week

Sep 11–17 Dating & Life Coach Recognition Week, National Assisted Living Week

Sep 12–17 National Line Dance Week

Sep 17–23 Constitution Week

Sep 17–18 Levi Coffin Days

Sep 18–24 Build a Better Image Week, International Clean Hands Week, National Farm Safety and Health Week, National Historically Black Colleges and Universities Week, National Rehabilitation Awareness Celebration Week, National Singles Week, Prostate Cancer Awareness Week, Tolkien Week, World Reflexology Week

Sep 19–25 Balance Awareness Week, International Week of the Deaf, International Women's eCommerce Days

Sep 23–25 Baltimore Book Festival

Sep 26–Oct 1 Banned Books Week—Celebrating the Freedom to Read

DAILY HOLIDAYS

1. *Chicken Boy's Birthday, *Edgar Rice Burroughs (1875) *Emma M. Nutt Day, International Toy Tips Executive Toy Test Day, Orthodox Ecclesiastical New Year, Slovakia: Constitution Day, Titanic Discovery Day

2. *Bison–Ten Yell Day, Calendar Adjustment Day, US Treasury Department Founded Day, *V–J Day

3. Penny Press Day (1833), Qatar: Independence Day, San Marino: National Day

4. Curacao: Animal's Day, Electric Lights Day, *Newspaper Carrier Day, *Paul Harvey Day

5. Be Late for Something Day, Canada & US: Labor Day (first Monday in September), Great Bathtub Race Day, Mackinac Bridge Walk, United Nations: International Day of Charity

6. Jane Addams Day, Swaziland: Independence Day, United Nations: Millennium Summit (1955)

7. Brazil: Independence Day, *Google Commemoration Day (1998), *Grandma Moses Day, *Neither Snow nor Rain Day–Day

8. Huey P. Long Shot Day, Pediatric Hematology/Oncology Nurses Day, Tarzan Day, *United Nations: International Literacy Day

9. *Bonza Bottler Day™, Japan: Chrysanthemum Day, National Day of Prayer and Remembrance, Tajikistan: Independence Day, *Wonderful Weirdoes Day

10. Prairie Day, World Suicide Prevention Day

11. *Attack on America Day, Ethiopia: New Year's Day, *Food Stamps Day, National Grandparents' Day, National Hug Your Hound Day, *Patriot Day and National Day of Service and Remembrance

12. Defenders Day, National Boss/Employee Exchange Day, United Nations: Day for South-South Cooperation

13. Kids Take Over the Kitchen Day, *National Celiac Awareness Day, Roald Dahl Day, Scooby Doo Day, United Nations: Opening Day of General Assembly

14. *Solo Transatlantic Balloon Crossing (1984)

15. *Agatha Christie Day, Costa Rica: Independence Day, El Salvador: Independence Day, *First National Convention for Blacks (1830), *Greenpeace Day (1971), Guatemala: Independence Day, Honduras: Independence Day, Korea: Chusok, Nicaragua: Independence Day, Quarterly Estimated Federal Income Tax Payers' Due Date (also Jan 15, Apr 15, June 15, and Sep 15, 2015), United Kingdom: Battle of Britain Day, *United Nations: International Day of Democracy

16. *Anne Bradstreet Day, Cherokee Strip Day, *Constitution / Pledge Across America Day, General Motors Day, *Great Seal of the US (1782), King Turkey Day, Mayflower Day, Mexico: Independence Day, National POW/MIA Recognition (the third Friday in September), National Tradesmen Day, Papua New Guinea: Independence Day, *United Nations: International Day for the Preservation of the Ozone Layer, World Play-Doh Day

17. AKC Responsible Dog Ownership Day, Big Whopper Liars Day, *Citizenship Day, *Constitution Day (1787), International Coastal Cleanup Day, Locate a Friend Day, National Constitution Center Constitution Day, National Football League Formed Day (1920), VFW Ladies Auxiliary Day

18. Chili: Independence Day, National HIV/AIDS and Aging Awareness Day, *US Air Force Birthday, *US Capitol Cornerstone Laid, White Woman Made American Indian Chief Day

19. *"Iceman" Mummy Discovered (1991), *International Talk Like A Pirate Day, Japan: Respect for the Aged Day, St Christopher (Saint Kitts) and Nevis: Independence Day

20. *National Equal Rights Founded (1884)

21. Armenia: Independence Day, Belize: Independence Day, Malta: Independence Day, National School Backpack Awareness Day, *United Nations: International Day of Peace

22. America Business Women's Day, Dear Diary Day, *Emancipation Proclamation (1862), Hobbit Day, Ice Cream Cone Day, International Day of Radiant Peace, Little Brown Jug Day, Long Count Day (1927), Mabon (Alban Elfed), Mali: Independence Day, National Centarian's Day, National Walk 'n' Roll Dog Day, US Postmaster General's Day (225th Anniversary)

23. Baseball's Greatest Dispute Day, *Celebrate Bisexuality Day, Checkers Day, Innergize Day, *Lewis & Clark Expedition Returns (1806), Planet Neptune Discovery (1846)

24. Everybody's Day Festival, Family Health and Fitness Day–USA, Fish Amnesty Day, Guinea-Bissau: Independence Day, National Hunting and Fishing Day, National Public Lands Day, *National Punctuation Day, R.E.A.D. in America Day, *Schwenkfelder Thanksgiving

25. *First American Newspaper Published (1690), Gold Star Mother's and Family Day, *Greenwich Mean Time Begins (1676), International Day of the Deaf, *National One-Hit Wonder Day, Pacific Ocean Discovered (1513), United Nations: World Maritime Day

26. *Johnny Appleseed Day, Family Day—Be Involved, Stay Involved™ Day

27. *Ancestor Appreciation Day, *Samuel Adams (1722), Saint Vincent DePaul Feast Day, *World Tourism Day

28. *Cabrillo Day, National Women's Health & Fitness Day, Taiwan: Confucius and Teachers' Day, World Rabies Day

29. Dow Jones Biggest Drop Day, International Coffee Day, *Michelangelo Antonioni (1912), Michaelmas, *National Attend Your Grandchild's Birth Day, National Biscotti Day, Scotland Yard Day (1829), Veterans of Foreign Wars Day

30. Botswana: Independence Day, Buffalo Roundup Day, Gutenberg Bible Published (1452), Hug A Vegan Day, International Translation Day

HOLIDAY MARKETING IDEAS FOR SEPTEMBER

Fall Hat Month—Did you know that this Weird & Wacky Holiday was a result of the fashion industry? The straw hat is out and the fabric or felt hat is officially in season! So now let's look at activities that could be enjoyed that celebrate hats. What about a "Mad Hatter Tea Party"? Have your guests wear their most unusual hat.

If you schedule a reading of a cat themed book at a library or even on-line, you are sure to please the children. Besides the standard *Cat in the Hat* series one set that comes to mind is *Max and Myron* series by Wendy VanHatten. You'll find the link to her books in the Resources. If you are so inclined you can always go to Amazon and search 'hats' under books and you will find several there. Once you know the titles take the list to your library and see what you can find there to read. Again, don't forget to mention that their silliest fall hat is requested be worn.

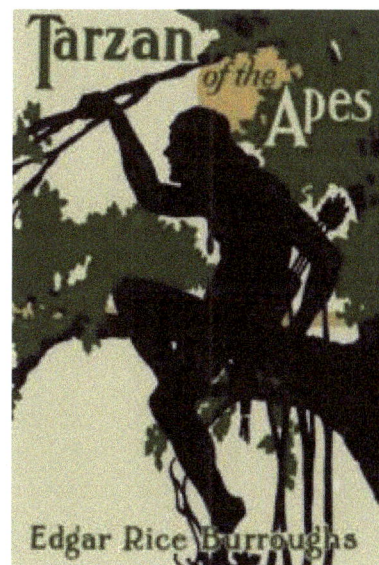

If you want to do something easy try a month-long Twitter campaign or send out hat themed notes or postcards to your customer/client list. This can easily be done from the comfort of your computer chair.

Sep 8 Tarzan Day—How much do you know about Tarzan? Why not share some interesting facts that you can easily dig up with others in a Twitter campaign today or even have a contest to see who can come up with the correct answers to questions written around the facts you uncover? Start a Facebook Tarzan Day group to easily host your event. You'll find a few tidbits in the appendix to get you started. In the resources you will find a *Fun Trivia* link to a whole lot more trivia questions you can use.

Sep 16 King Turkey Day—Today join in the festivities of the 77ᵗʰ Annual King Turkey Day celebration. 'Wild Turkey' races and pancakes are a tradition that you too can incorporate into your festivities. Dress up as turkeys and have a Turkey Parade or even have your own charity Turkey Trot.

If you can't think of anything else, a Left-Over Turkey Recipe Swap would be an easily done activity. After all, Thanksgiving is just around the corner. Nevertheless, if you think about it, I am sure you will come up with several fun activities you can do on this Weird & Wacky Holiday. Check out the official King Turkey Day website for additional information on what they are doing to celebrate today. You will find the link in the resources.

Courtesy of www.gwlittle.com

Sep 21 National School Backpack Awareness Day—Across the country, backpack events educate parents, students, educators and school administrators, and communities about the serious health effects that backpacks that are too heavy or worn improperly have on children. Backpack Day is also a time to promote the full range of occupational therapy benefits and services. So if you are in a health/fitness field or in a childcare/educational career, this Weird & Wacky Holiday should be on your horizon.

The American Occupational Therapy Association, Inc has a wonderful poster on their website for your display and plenty of event ideas and artwork. Be sure to check it out in the resources section of this book. I have included a few in the appendix to make it easy for you to access.

Set 28 World Rabies Day—Today we are to inform and educate about this horrendous disease that has a death rate of nearly 100%! However, it has become easy to prevent with safe and modern vaccines. With the knowledge that more than 95% of cases are in victims from Asia to Africa it is your chance to do what you can to help bring awareness of the issues surrounding rabies and its prevention.

Get involved, raise funds, raise awareness, and help end the devastating disease called Rabies! When you join with your community, or even on-line, you can make a difference while making others aware of your business by participating or sponsoring a drive or event.

OCTOBER

MONTH-LONG HOLIDAYS

Oct 15–Nov 30 Wishbone for Pets Days

Oct 24–Nov 11 World Origami Days

Adopt A Shelter Dog Month, American Cheese Month, Antidepressant Death Awareness Month, Breast Cancer Awareness Month, Caffeine Addiction Recovery Month, Celebrating The Bilingual Child Month, Celiac Disease Awareness Month, Church Library Month, Co–op Awareness Month, Cut Out Dissection Month, Domestic Violence Awareness Month, Dyslexia Awareness Month, Emotional Intelligence Month, Gay & Lesbian History Month, German–American Heritage Month, Global Diversity Awareness Month, Go Hog Wild—Eat Country Ham Month, Health Literacy Month, Home Eye Safety Month, National Arts and Humanities Month, National Audiology Awareness Month, National Bake and Decorate Month, National Breast Cancer Awareness Month, National Bullying Prevention Awareness Month, National Chiropractic Month, National Crime Prevention Month, National Critical Illness Awareness Month, National Cyber Security Awareness Month, National Dental Hygiene Month, National Depression Education & Awareness Month, National Disability Employment Awareness Month, National Domestic Violence Awareness Month, National Down Syndrome Awareness Month, National "Gain The Inside Advantage" Month, National Kitchen and Bath Month, National Liver Awareness Month, National Medical Librarian Month, National Orthodontic Health Month, National Physical Therapy Month, National Popcorn Poppin' Month, National Reading Group Month, National Roller Skating Month, National Spina Bifida Awareness Month, National Stamp Collecting Month, National Stop Bullying Month, National Work and Family Month, Organize Your Medical Information Month, Polish American Heritage Month, Positive Attitude Month, Rett Syndrome Awareness Month, Right–Brainers Rule Month, Spinach Lovers Month, Squirrel Awareness & Appreciation Month, Talk About Prescriptions Month, Vegetarian Month, Workplace Politics Awareness Month, World Menopause Month

WEEK-LONG HOLIDAYS

Oct 2–8 Mental Illness Awareness Week, Mystery Series Week, National Carry a Tune Week, National Chimney Safety Week, National Work from Home Week, Nuclear Medicine and Molecular Imaging Week

Oct 3–7 Kids' Goal Setting Week, National Heimlich Heroes Week

Oct 4–10 United Nations: World Space Week

Oct 6–9 Dalton Defenders Day

Oct 7–9 Apple Butter Makin' Days, Come and Take It Celebration

Oct 8–10 Chowder Days

Oct 9–15 Death Penalty Focus Week, Emergency Nurses Week, Fire Prevention Week, Getting the World to Beat a Path to Your Door Week, National Metric Week

Oct 10–14 National School Lunch Week

Oct 10–16 World Rainforest Week

Oct 10–17 Take Your Medicine Americans Week

Oct 13-27 Chicago International Film Festival

Oct 15–20 Japan: Newspaper Week

Oct 16–22 Bullying Bystanders Unite Week, National Character Counts Week, National Chemistry Week, National Food Bank Week, National Forest Products Week, National Friends of Libraries Week, Teen Read Week

Oct 17–21 National School Bus Safety Week

Oct 17–23 Sukkot, Succoth or Feast of Tabernacles

Oct 17–24 Food and Drug Interaction Education and Awareness Week

Oct 19–23 Germany: Frankfurt Book Fair

Oct 23–29 National Massage Therapy Awareness Week®, Pastoral Care Week, Rodent Awareness Week

Oct 24–28 National Nuclear Science Week

Oct 24–30 United Nations: Disarmament Week

Oct 24–31 Prescription Errors Education & Awareness Week

Oct 25–31 International Magic Week

DAILY HOLIDAYS

1. CyberSpace Day, Cyprus: Independence Day, Disney World Opened (1971), *Fire Pup Day, Model-T Day, National Book It! Day, Nigeria: Independence Day, South Korea: Armed Forces Day, *United Nations: International Day of Older Persons, Vegan Baking Day, Woofstock, World Vegetarian Day

2. Blessing of the Fishing Fleet, Country Inn / Bed–and–Breakfast Day, *Guardian Angels Day, *Groucho Marx (1890), Guinea: Independence Day, Islamic New Year, *National Custodial Workers Day, *"Peanuts" Debut Day (1950), *Phileas Fogg's Wager Day, Rosh Hashanah (begins at sundown), United Nations: International Day of Nonviolence, World Communion Sunday, *World Day for Farm Animals

3. Blue Shirt Day™, Child Health Day (always issued for the first Monday in October), Germany: Day of German Unity, Korea: Tangun Day (National Foundation Day), *Mickey Mouse Club Day (1955), Rosh Hashanah or Jewish New Year (3–4), United Nations: World Habitat Day

4. *Dick Tracy Day (1931), *Georgian Calendar Adjustment Day, National Ships-In-Bottles Day, St Francis of Assisi: Feast Day, *Ten-Four Day

5. Fast of Gedalya, Portugal: Republic Day, *United Nations: World Teachers Day

6. *American Library Association Founding Day (1876), Egypt: Armed Forces Day, Ireland: Ivy Day, *Jackie Mayer Rehab Day, National Depression Screening Day, *National German-American Day, Yom Kippur War

7. Canada: Kitchener-Waterloo Oktoberfest, National Diversity Day, World Smile Day

8. *Alvin C. York Day, Fall Astronomy Day, *Great Chicago Fire (1871), Monster Myths by Moonlight, National Pierogy Day, Universal Music Day

9. China: Chung Yeung Festival (Double Nine), Grandmother's Day in Florida, Korea: Hangul (Alphabet Day), *Leif Erickson Day, Samoa and American Samoa: White Sunday, Uganda: Independence Day, *United Nations: World Post Day

10. American Indian Heritage Day, *Bonza Bottler Day™, Canada: Thanksgiving Day, Columbus Day (Observed & Traditional),*Double 10 Day, Fiji: Independence Day, Discovery Day in Hawaii, Japan: Health–Sports Day, National Handbag Day, National Kick Butt Day, Native Americans' Day, *Tuxedo Day, *US Naval Academy Day, World Day Against the Death Penalty, *World Mental Health Day, Yorktown Victory Day

11. ADA Lovelace Day, Ashura: Tenth Day, *Adding Machine Day, *General Pulaski Memorial Day, India: Dasara (Dussehra), *National Coming Out Day, National Face Your Fears Day, Southern Food Heritage Day, United Nations: International Day of the Girl Child, Yom Kippur (begins at sundown)

12. Bahamas Discovery Day, Belize: Columbus Day, Columbus Day (Traditional), *Day of the Six–Billion, Emergency Nurses Day, Freethought Day, *International Moment of Frustration Scream Day, International Top Spinning Day, Mexico: Dia de la Raza, National Bring Your Teddy Bear To Work Day, National Stop Bullying Day, National Take Your Parents to Lunch Day, Yom Kippur or Day of Atonement

13. *Leroy Brown Day, *Navy Birthday, Silly Sayings Day, United Nations: International Day for Natural Disaster Reduction

14. *Be Bald and Be Free Day

15. Blind Americans Equality Day (formerly White Cane Safety Day), Bridge Day, National Cake Decorating Day, National Grouch Day, National Latino AIDS Awareness Day, Sweetest Day (third Saturday), United Nations: International Day of Rural Women

16. Department Store Day, Dictionary Day, Birth Control Day (1916), Sukkot (begins at sundown), United Nations: World Food Day

17. 300 Millionth American Born (2006), Black Poetry Day, Jamaica: National Heroes Day, *Mulligan Day, *National Boss' Day, San Francisco 1989 Earthquake (1989), *United Nations: International Day for the Eradication of Poverty

18. Alaska Day, Canada: Persons Day, Comic Strip Day, St Luke Feast Day, Water Pollution Control Day, *World Menopause Day

19. Evaluate Your Life Day, Hagfish Day, LGBT Center Awareness Day, Missouri Day, Yorktown Day

20. *Australia: Sydney Opera House Day, Get to Know Your Customers Day (third Thursday of each quarter is set aside to get to know your customers even better), Get Smart About Credit Day, Miss America Rose Day

21. *Incandescent Lamp Day, National Mammography Day, *Samuel "Crash Test Dummy" Alderson Day (1914)

22. *International Stuttering Awareness Day, Make a Difference Day, Smart is Cool Day, World's End Day

23. Hungary: Republic Day (Declairs Independence), *IPod Day, Mother-in-Law Day, National Mole Day, Swallows Depart from San Juan Capistrano

24. New Zealand: Labor Day, Shemini Atzeret, United Nations Day, *United Nations: World Development Information Day, Zambia: Independence Day

25. St Crispin's Day, Simchat Torah

26. Austria: National Day, Erie Canal Day, Mule Day

27. *Cranky Coworkers Day, *Navy Day, Saint Vincent and the Grenadines: Independence Day, United Nations: World Day for Audiovisual Heritage, *Walt Disney Day

28. Czech Republic: Independence Day, Frankenstein Friday, Greece: Ochi Day, *St Jude's Day, Statue of Liberty Dedication (1886)

29. *Internet Created (1969), National Cat Day, National Forgiveness Day

30. A Family Halloween Day, Checklists Day, *Create A Great Funeral Day, Devil's Night, *Emily Post Day, *Haunted Refrigerator Night, India: Diwali (Deepavali), National Candy Corn Day, Reformation Sunday, "War of the Worlds" (1938)

31. *Books For Treats Day, *Halloween, *Magic Day, *National Knock–Knock Day, *Reformation Day, Samhain, Nevada Day Celebration, Trick or Treat or Beggar's Night, United Nations: World Cities Day

HOLIDAY MARKETING IDEAS FOR OCTOBER

National Popcorn Poppin' Month—Popcorn is one of our national foods. Not only is it yummy, but it is actually healthy for you, too. Whether you celebrate with recipe swaps or grabbing a bag of sweet Kettle Corn—my favorite—and savoring the flavor you are sure to enjoy this national Weird & Wacky Holiday.

But ... don't stop there! Think about how you can use this holiday to create a Poppin' Event. What about hosting a poppin' good, fast and furious, info laden event? This is simple to do on-line if you can take the heat. Sorry, I couldn't help myself. *wink* Fundraisers are another way to share the love of popcorn this month. Find a charity of choice or a school who would appreciate your efforts and you'll sell a ton of popcorn at your charity event or auction. Oh, and don't forget to let the media know what you are up to. As I have mentioned before, the media loves feel-good events!

Are you hungry for some popcorn recipes or facts? Check out a few provided by none other than Popcorn.org in the appendix. And, keep looking 'cuz the Popcorn Infogram is there as well.

Oct 2–8 National Carry a Tune Week—Here's a wonderful marketing opportunity for your business especially if you are a speaking coach or other vocal trainer. You could offer up short video clips throughout the week emphasizing on proper breathing techniques and other vocal warm-ups that anyone who wants to become a public speaker should know and use.

Or you could have a 'Name That Tune' event and contest on-line or off-line. Either way that could be a whole lot of fun. I can even see Twitter being used for vocal tips or any fun musical oldie but goodie tune that you can remember.

Oct 2 Guardian Angels Day—Today we celebrate those among us that have made a significant impact on our lives. While they may still be present in body that doesn't take away from their sainthood. Find a special way to thank them for their prayers, guidance, and support. If they happen to be elderly, give them a call today, take them to lunch, or just share a note of thanks with a specific remembrance that will light up their day. You will find this angel on a postcard that you are welcome to use in the appendix.

If a live and in person visit is not possible due to distance, pick up the phone and give them a call. No matter if they are a mentor, parent, or friend, they will be both pleased and rewarded by your selfless act.

Oct 4 Dick Tracy Day—Dick Tracy was yesterday what a pop icon would be to the kids today. He was popularized by Chester Gould debuting on this day back in 1931. His motto: Law and Order, FIRST. Now that you know the facts ma'am, let's put our thinking caps on and uncover how to create the buzz for your business around this Weird & Wacky Holiday.

Here's one. How about rooting out the bad habits we try to keep hidden? Why not put together a group on-line or off and have speakers share or have round table discussions. Bad habits are hard to crack, but things like procrastination and even smoking are number one on the list. Check the appendix for a poster to get you on the case.

Are you an artist? Why not try working with the younger generation and helping them stave off a life of crime using bad drawing or painting techniques. This would work just as well for writers at a writer or author

conference. Are you a health professional? Shoot, this type of event I can't think of even one profession that wouldn't benefit from having a workshop geared around their customers, clients, and patients. If you are in law enforcement or the legal system, well, you certainly don't have an alibi that will stand up in court!

Oct 8 Great Chicago Fire—This is a great of an opportunity to set your world ablaze. Fire, of course would be your theme of the day and taking action would be the spark to ignite that flame. While the flames of progress lap at your mind and consume your imagination, consider hosting an event that will burn up the Internet. Get some sponsors and speakers who can share on marketing and sales and even on Autorepsonders. There are many topics that would be a perfect fit for this type of event. Press release writing and even employment companies that offer resume writing and proper dress and etiquette on job interviews would fire up interest in your event.

Start early to promote your event and fan the flames with cross-promotional efforts and you will certainly light a fire in the lives of the masses.

Oct 10 Tuxedo Day—Since I know there are some of you that are career oriented coaches and trainers I couldn't pass up the chance to focus on this Weird & Wacky Holiday. Today is all about looking and feeling your best. Oh my, that just opened the door for exercise coaches and health professionals too! A tips card or Tweets or even an event focused around this theme will do wonders for your marketing.

Then there are those who offer 'feel good' products like bath products, candles, and even makeup that could benefit from focusing on Tuxedo Day events or sales. Put your thinking cap on and see what you can come up with to garner the attention of the media and your adoring fans.

Oct 13 Silly Sayings Day—You know all those inane saying you have heard all your life like, spill the beans, hold your horses, and it's raining cats and dogs? Well today is the day to celebrate those that we have seen go the way of the dead horse and those we still use today. Have a fun day seeing how many you can come up with and use in your conversations. Then when the good folks look at you like the cat that just swallowed a canary you can laugh along with them.

Do you even know where these silly sayings originated? It might be fun to look them up and try to let the cat out of the bag.

Courtesy of NOAA Okeanos Explorer Program

Oct 19 Hagfish Day—Today we celebrate the beauty in even the most ugliest of sea creatures. So, as you think about ways to market your wares consider events and opportunities that show tolerance and understanding for those around us. Just because another person doesn't look or act like you do is no reason to think less of them.

As in nature, beauty isn't everything—and in fact, the Hagfish is a

highly evolved and specialized creature worthy of respect. So, celebrate the joy of diversity rather than sameness not just today, but everyday.

WhaleTimes (http://whaletimes.org/?cat=2) has a few suggestions on how to celebrate the 'beauty of ugly' so here are some fun activities. Try making your own hagfish slime or perhaps make a gorgeous Hagfish Day Bouquet for a friend or even write a Hagfish Haiku, or make a Slime Time Crown and become Hagfish Day Royalty. The recipe for Hagfish Day Slime is in the appendix. These are great with kids, but for businesses you could send out some Happy Hagfish Day cards or tweet using the hashtag #hagfish for starters.

NOVEMBER

MONTH-LONG HOLIDAYS

Nov 6, 2016–Mar 12, 2017 Daylight Saving Time Ends

Nov 26–Dec 4 Mexico: Guadalajara International Book Fair

Aviation History Month, Banana Pudding Lovers Month, Diabetic Eye Disease Month, Lung Cancer Awareness Month, Movember, National Adoption Month, National Alzheimer's Disease Awareness Month, National Diabetes Month, National Epilepsy Awareness Month, National Family Caregivers Month, National Georgia Pecan Month, National Inspirational Role Models Month, National Long–Term Care Awareness Month, National Marrow Awareness Month, National Memoir Writing Month, National Native American Heritage Month, National Novel Writing Month, Peanut Butter Lovers Month, Picture Book Month, PPSI AIDS Awareness Month, Prematurity Awareness Month, Vegan Month, Worldwide Bereaved Siblings Month

WEEK-LONG HOLIDAYS

Nov 2–13 Edgar Allan Poe Evermore

Nov 7–11 National Young Reader's Week

Nov 11–13 National Donor Sabbath

Nov 13–20 Miami Book Fair International

Nov 14–18 American Education Week

Nov 14–20 National Book Awards Week

Nov 20–26 National Family Week, National Game & Puzzle Week™

Nov 20–27 International Bible Week

Nov 21–25 Church/State Separation Week

Nov 21–27 Better Conversation Week

DAILY HOLIDAYS

1. *All Hallows or All Saints Day, Antigua and Barbuda Independence Day, Birth of the Bab (1–2), European Union (1993), Extra Mile Day, Hockey Mask Day, Mexico: Day of the Dead, *National Authors' Day, National Cook for Your Pets Day

2. *All Souls Day, *First Scheduled Radio Broadcast (1920), National Traffic Directors Day, *Plan Your Epitaph Day, United Nations: International Day to End Impunity for Crimes Against Journalists

3. *Cliché Day, *Japan: Culture Day, National Men Make Dinner Day, Panama: Independence Day, Public Television Day, *Sandwich Day, SOS Day

4. *Italy: Victory Day, *King Tut Tomb Discovery (1922), Mischief Night, *National Chicken Lady Day, National Medical Science Liaison Awareness and Appreciation Day,* Panama: Flag Day, Punkin Chunkin Day, Russia: Unity Day, UNESCO Day, *Will Rogers (1879)

5. *England: Guy Fawkes Day, Pumpkin Destruction Day, *Roy Rogers (1911), Sadie Hawkins Day, *Shattered Backboard Day, Vivian Leigh–Scarlett O'Hara Day (1913)

6. Saxophone Day, *United Nations: International Day for Preventing the Exploitation of the Environment in War and Armed Conflict, Zero Tasking Day

7. Australia: Recreation Day, Fill Your Staplers Day, First Black Governor Elected (1989), Job Action Day

8. Abet and Aid Punsters Day, Cook Something Bold and Pungent Day, General Election Day, *National Parents As Teachers Day, *X–ray Day

9. *Berlin Wall Opened (1989), Cambodia: Independence Day, Germany: Kristallnacht, National Child Safety Council Day

10. *Area Code Day (1951), Marine Corps Day, Claude Rains Day, Return Day

11. Angola: Independence Day, *Bonza Bottler Day™, Canada: Remembrance Day, Columbia: Cartagena Independence Day, Death/Duty Day, England: Remembrance Day, God Bless America Day, Japan: Origami Day, Martinmas, Poland: Independence Day, Sweden: St Martin's Day, Switzerland: Martinmas Goose (Martinigians), *Veterans Day

12. Mexico: Postman's Day, World Pneumonia Day

13. Germany: Volkstrauertag, Holland Tunnel Day

14. India: Children's Day, International Girls Day, Loosen Up Lighten Up Day, Moby Dick Day, Claude Monet Day, Spirit of NSA (National Speakers Association) Day, *United Nations: World Diabetes Day, World Orphans Day

15. *America Recycles Day, Belgium: Dynasty Day, Brazil: Republic Day, George Spelvin Day, Japan: Shichi–Go–San, *National Bundt (Pan) Day

16. Germany: Buss Und Bettag, *Lewis and Clark Expedition Reaches Pacific Ocean (1805), National Educational Support Professionals Day, *United Nations: International Day for Tolerance

17. Great American Smoke-out (third Thursday), *Homemade Bread Day, National Unfriend Day, World Philosophy Day, World Prematurity Day

18. Latvia: Independence Day, *Married to a Scorpio Support Day, *Mickey Mouse's Birthday (1928), Substitute Educators Day

19. Alascattalo Day (About Alaska & humor), Belize: Garifuna Day, *Dedication Day (1862), Gettysburg: Remembrance Day, *"Have A Bad Day" Day, International Games Day, Puerto Rico: Discovery Day

20. *Bill of Rights Day, Germany: Totensonntag, Edwin Powell Hubble Day, *Madelbrot Day (1924), Mexico: Revolution Day, *Name Your PC Day, Transgender Day of Remembrance, *United Nations: African Industrialization Day, United Nations: Universal Children's Day, United Nations: World Day of Remembrance for Road Traffic Victims

21. *Sir Samuel Cunard (1787), *United Nations: World Television Day, World Hello Day

22. Charles DeGaulle Day 1890), *George Eliot (1819), Humane Society of the US Day (1954)

23. Billy the Kid Day, Fibonacci Day, Tie One On Day™

24. *Celebrate Your Unique Talent Day, *Dale Carnegie (1888),*D.B. Cooper Day, Thanksgiving Day, Turkey-free Thanksgiving Day

25. *Andrew Carnegie (1835), Black Friday, *Bosnia and Herzegovina: National Day, Buy Nothing Day, Family Day in Nevada, *JFK Day (1960), National Flossing Day, Native American Heritage Day, St Catherine's Day, *Shopping Reminder Day, Sinkie Day, Suriname: Independence Day, United Nations: International Day For the Elimination of Violence Against Women Day

26. Charles Schultz (1922), *Eric Sevareid (1912), International Aura Awareness Day, Small Business Saturday

27. Advent Sunday, Face Transplant Day, Handel's Messiah Sing-Along

28. *Albania: Independence Day (1912), Cider Monday, Cyber Monday, *Lévi–Strauss (1908), Mauritania: Independence Day, Panama: Independence from Spain, Switzerland: Zibelemarit (Onion Market)

29. *CS Lewis (1898), *Electronic Greetings Day, Giving Tuesday, *United Nations: International Day of Solidarity With The Palestinian People

30. Barbados: Independence Day, *Computer Security Day, St Andrew's Day, *Statue of Ramses II Unearthed (1991), *Stay Home Because You're Well Day

HOLIDAY MARKETING IDEAS FOR NOVEMBER

Aviation History Month—Today we celebrate the first hot air balloon which was the beginning of aviation as we now know it. Okay, I hear you saying, but I'm not into airplanes. Well, you certainly know about how to be the wind beneath other's wings, as Bette Midler sings. You could choose to focus on coaching or training with this theme or go the route of hot air either blowing up or letting out steam. If you opt for the release of steam you could tackle subjects such as anger management, customer service issues, or relaxation techniques. These are just the first few that come to my mind. You can take it from there and soar!

Nov 1 Hockey Mask Day—This is such a good one that it bears reuse this year too. (Check out the 2014 Edition for additional suggestions and tools.) As you probably guessed Canada takes the puck for the invention of the hockey mask. But, for your business to thrive you need to market it in ways that will make you stand out from the crowd. Hockey Mask Day might just be everything you've been looking for. As you celebrate this Weird & Wacky Holiday look at it from the realm of protection; self-, Internet, financial, or even loss of your dream. Find ways to share information on ways to protect your customers and clients from any number of maladies, maybe even health concerns. You'll find a poster to get you started in the appendix.

No matter what you do, whether sending out cards or hosting events, this is one day you will be glad you made the effort and got your name back in front of those potential and current clients and customers.

Nov 3 SOS Day—Raise your flag for distress today in your marketing efforts. Look for ways to help others out of jams or help them help themselves. What if today could change everything for someone you know? Wouldn't you want to be there for them? Be absolutely certain to check out the official website for more information and make this a significant day in the life of you, your business, and others.

With famous people like Abba and Will Smith aligning with this Weird & Wacky Holiday, you will make a big splash in the media when you use this day to market your business in ways that will make the media take notice. They say on their website, "If you would like to help host, present, partner or participate in a live physical event near you please contact your relevant referring participant or partner, mentor or relationship manager." You'll find the link to their website in the resources section.

PEA TOWNSHEND: Pete Townshend pea guitarist The Who vegetable

Nov 8 Abet and Aid Punsters Day—Today we laugh instead of groan at the horrendously bad puns that abound around us. Did you know that there is actually a resister of worst puns? Check 'em out at Punsters Unlimited, if you can find them. Otherwise, while you are trying to come up with a few of your own, why not add an image to your madness? Here's one from Foodlebrities.com that I couldn't pass up sharing.

Columnist Doug Larson once said, "A pun is the lowest form of humor, unless you thought of it yourself." So, today have yourself a punning good time. Try to come up with an original pun or two and share them in tweets with the hashtag #punstersday. But, don't get overly 'pundent' and remember, "The pun also rises."

Nov 14 Orphans Day—Imagine being orphaned, finding yourself alone and unloved. Now, turn your mind to the hope that one day a year YOU are celebrated; special. Today you can make a difference in the life of not just one but all orphans. Give of your time and talent. Visit an orphanage in your home town to learn about what it is like from their perspective. Organize a group to go with you and share your love and talents with them.

Organize an ice cream social and make them kings and queens for the day. Use the funds from your ice cream social to help raise awareness, support, and funding for motherless and fatherless children worldwide. When you do, make sure the media knows what you are up to you. If you are in need of a little help, I would be more than happy to work with you on this marketing plan. Just let me know and I'll chime in where I can.

Nov 26 International Aura Awareness Day—Whether you believe in auras or not, this Weird & Wacky Holiday can be used to market your business by considering the impact we have on those around us. So, raise your audience's awareness of your business by giving them insight into how they too can touch those closest to them in a positive way. Whether that is training them or just spending time with them, let them know you care enough to share this special holiday with them.

If you have a book or business on this subject or one of spiritual value this is a great day to schedule a presentation, reading, or even a book signing. If you need a venue, check out your local library. They often have rooms to host these types of events.

Nov 29 Electronic Greetings Day—This is certainly a day we as business owners should add to our pack of marketing plans. I don't think much needs to be said, other than 'Just Do It!' You will find a whole host of Electronic Greeting Card Companies in the resources. However, you aren't limited to the use of cards, an email note will suffice if you don't see one that is to your liking.

DECEMBER

MONTH-LONG HOLIDAYS

Dec 17–Feb 5, 2017 Take a New Year's Resolution to Stop Smoking (TANYRSS)

Bingo's Birthday Month, National Impaired Driving Prevention Month, National Write a Business Plan Month, Safe Toys and Gifts Month, Worldwide Food Service Safety Month

WEEK-LONG HOLIDAYS

Dec 1–17 Operation Santa Paws

Dec 3–10 Clerc-Gallaudet Week

Dec 5–9 Cookie Exchange Week

Dec 14–Jan 5, 2017 Christmas Bird Count

Dec 14–28 Halcyon Days

Dec 16–25 Philippines: Simbang Gabi

Dec 17–23 Saturnalia

Dec 25–Jan 1, 2017 Chanukah

Dec 26–Jan 1, 2017 Kwanzaa

DAILY HOLIDAYS

1. Antarctica Day, *Basketball Day, *Bifocals at the Monitor Liberation Day, *Civil Air Patrol Day, Day With(out) Art, National Christmas Tree Lighting, Portugal: Independence Day, Rosa Parks Day, *United Nations: World AIDS Day

2. *Artificial Heart Transplant Day (1967), England: Walter Plinge Day, *Joseph Bell (1837), National Sales Person's Day, *Safety Razor Day, *Special Education Day, United Arab Emirates: Independence Day, *United Nations: International Day for the Abolition of Slavery Day

3. First Heart Transplant (1967), *United Nations: International Day of Persons with Disabilities

4. Mary Celeste Discovery Day, *Samuel Butler (1835), St Barbara's Day

5. *AFL–CIO Founded (1955), Austria: Krampuslauf, *Bathtub Party Day, "Irrational Exuberance" Day, Montgomery Bus Boycott Remembrance Day, *United Nations: International Volunteer Day for Economic & Social Development, United Nations: World Soil Day, *Walt Disney (1901)

6. *National Miners' Day, *National Pawnbrokers Day, *St Nicholas Day

7. Iran: Students Day, *National Fire Safety Council Founding (1979), *National Pearl Harbor Remembrance Day, Special Kids Day, *United Nations: International Civil Aviation Day

8. *Eli Whitney (1765), Feast of Immaculate Conception, Intermediate-Range Nuclear Forces Treaty (INF) Signed (1987), NAFTA Day, Soviet Union Dissolved (1991)

9. Official Lost and Found Day, *United Nations: International Anti-Corruption Day

10. *Ada Lovelace (1815), *Dewey Decimal System Day, *Emily Dickenson (1830), Gingerbread Decorating Day, *Human Rights Day, National Day of the Horse, *Nobel Prize Day, *Thomas Hopkins Gallaudet (1787), *United Nations: Human Rights Day

11. *UNICEF Birthday, *United Nations: International Mountain Day

12. *Bonza Bottler Day™, Day of Our Lady of Guadalupe, Mexico: Guadalupe Day, *Poinsettia Day, *Puerto Rico: Las Mañanitas

13. *New Zealand Discovery (1642), Sweden: St Lucia Day

14. *Doolittle Day, Nostradamus (1503), South Pole Discovery (1911)

15. *Bill of Rights Day, *Cat Herders Day, Puerto Rico: Navidades

16. Bahrain: Independence Day, *Barbie and Barney Backlash Day, Boston Tea Party Day, *Jane Austen (1775), *Ludwig Van Beethoven (1770), Mexico: Posadas, Underdog Day, *United Nations: Zionism Day

17. *Azteck Calendar Stone Discovery Day (1790), *Clean Air Day, *Joseph Henry (1797), *Wright Brothers Day

18. *Benjamin O Davis, Jr. (1912), *Joseph Grimaldi (1778), Mexico: Feast of Our Lady of Solitude, *Antonio Stradivari Death (1737), *United Nations: International Migrants Day

19. Titanic Day

20. Cathode-Ray Tube Day, *Mudd Day, *United Nations: International Human Solidarity Day

21. *Heinrich Böll (1917), Celebrate Short Fiction Day, *Crossword Puzzle Day, *Forefathers Day, *Humbug Day, *Phileas Fogg Win A Wager Day, Pilgrim Landing, Yalda, Yule

22. First Gorilla Born in Captivity (1956), *Giacomo Puccini (1858), Oglethorpe Day

23. *Federal Reserve System (1913), HumanLight Celebration Day, Japan: Birthday of the Emperor, Metric Conversion Act (1975), Mexico: Feast of Radishes, *Transistor Day (1947)

24. Chanukah (begins at sundown), *Christmas Eve , *James Prescott Joule (1818), Libya: Independence Day

25. *A'Phabet Day or No-L-Day, *Christmas Day, Cuba: Christmas Returns, *Clara Barton (1821), *Evangeline Cory Booth (1865)

26. *Bahamas: Junkanoo, Boxing Day, Ireland: Day of the Wren, Luxembourg: Blessing of the Wine, *Mao Tse-Tung (1893), *National Whiner's Day, Radium Day, Second Day of Christmas, St Stephen's Day, Slovenia: Independence Day, South Africa: Day of Goodwill, *United Nations: Boxing Day

27. *Johannes Kepler (1571), *Louis Pasteur (1822), St John, Apostle-Evangelist: Feast Day

28. Australia: Proclamation Day, *Cinema Day, Endangered Species Day, *Holy Innocents Day or Childermas, *Pledge of Allegiance Day

29. Andrew Johnson Wreath-Laying, St Thomas of Canterbury: Feast Day, *Tick Tock Day, *YMCA Day

30. *Falling Needles Family Fest Day, *Rudyard Kipling (1865), No Interruptions Day, USSR DAY (1922)

31. *First Nights, *Japan: Namahage, *Leap Second Adjustment Time Day, *Make Up Your Mind Day, *New Year's Eve, New Year's Banished Words List, St Sylvester's Day, Scotland: Hogmany, *World Peace Meditation Day

HOLIDAY MARKETING IDEAS FOR DECEMBER

Dec 5–9 Cookie Exchange Week—This week is the kick-off to the Christmas holiday season. Take some time to bake some cookies, if you are into that sort of thing and have the time. If not, pick up a box of cookies from your grocery or specialty shop. Put a few in special boxes wrapped in wrapping paper and be sure to attach your business card or contact information to the ribbon along with a note letting the recipient know that you are a fan of this Weird & Wacky Holiday. You'll find a few of my favorite cookie recipes in the appendix.

Then, take them out and give them away. A local food bank is a good place to start, especially if you are doing this as a group. If you partner with a local restaurant you could make this a joint venture. Imagine the good will you will spread with the owner and their customers while getting your name in front of a group of folks you wouldn't normally have access to. This is certain to be a win/win/win for all involved. And if you have written a cookbook, you could even leave a fishbowl for business cards to win a copy of your book!

Another alternative is to create recipe cards with your logo on them and hand them out both on-line and in person, or mail them to your mailing lists. The best thing is, the recipient will be likely to keep your recipe card FOREVER!

Dec 2 Artificial Heart Transplant Day—Today we celebrate life and the life-giving extension before receiving a heart transplant. It is a very sophisticated device. So as you look to celebrate this Weird & Wacky Holiday think life-giving, life affirming, or even bridging the gap. These directions should spark your imagination as it does mine.

There are a few facts about heart transplants that you could put on a card with your logo and hand out if you are up to that. See the appendix for one you can use and check the resources where you will find the link to one life-giving heart transplant machine manufacturer, Syncardia. They have a lot of information on their website to further your knowledge on the subject.

However, you don't have to be in the medical field to promote your business today. There are lots of subjects you could cover in a teleconference, seminar, or webinar. Or you could just tweet away. Use this day wisely and you too will grow your business.

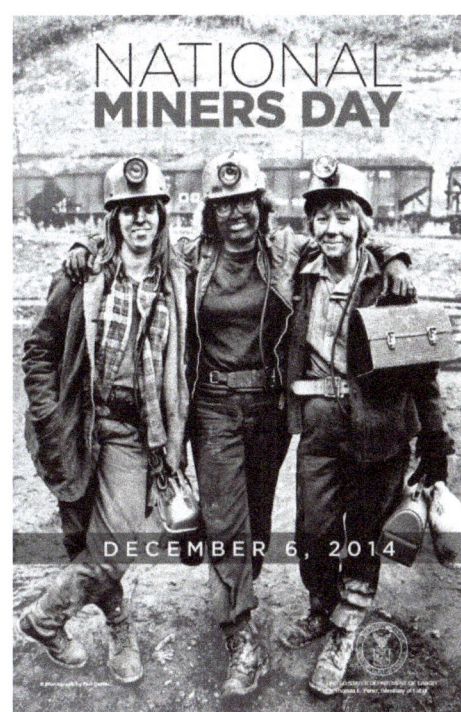

Dec 6 National Miners' Day—I know this is about supporting miners of all ores. However, to reach our goals we all must do a bit of mining first. Our number one priority is knowledge. Then comes ability or talent, and last good hard work and dedication. So, today your challenge is to see what you can remove from your mind and life that is standing in the way of your success. Then you will be able to continue to share in the blessing of those who love their work and do it with no fear of failure.

If you are already there, why not share with others how you managed to survive in a world where 60% are doomed to failure in their first four years in business. Yup, but you knew that, right?

Dec 10 National Day of the Horse—Horses have always been more than just beautiful, graceful beasts. They have been friend and workforce for many. Therefore, today we can focus on the support we receive from those who assist us in our endeavors. It is your opportunity to thank your lucky stars that your assistant, designer, co-worker, partner and friends have stood by you through it all.

Sending out small thank you gifts is probably the most efficient and effective use of your time today.

Courtesy of US Dpt of Labor Blog

Dec 17 Aztec Calendar Stone Discovery Day—Most of us remember the end of the world predictions caused by this famous stone unearthed in Mexico City. Nevertheless, the world still goes on, thriving and growing, discovering and learning. So today we should put aside our fears and look to a new age of discovery and success. As we near our Christmas holiday season perhaps the most appropriate thing we can do to promote our businesses is to send out ecards or tweets to remind everyone you know that while the calendar year is nearing its end, their need to discover ways to continue growing and building their successful empire is but a word or event away. Keep seeking, never give up, stay inspired.

"1479 Stein der fünften Sonne, sog. Aztekenkalender, Ollin Tonatiuh anagoria" by Anagoria - Own work. Licensed under CC BY 3.0 via Commons

Appendix A: SAMPLES

Sample Press Release

FOR IMMEDIATE RELEASE

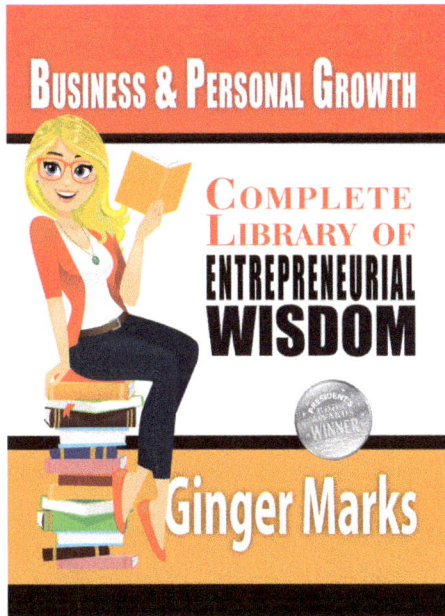

30+ YEAR LOCAL VETERAN BUSINESS OWNER / AUTHOR PARTNERS WITH PNC BANK

CLEARWATER, FL— SEPTEMBER 21, 2014 Local author and publisher, Ginger Marks, partners with Clearwater's PNC Bank to provide insight and advice for prospective, new, and experienced business owners. Ginger will be available to chat and sign copies of her award winning book, Complete Library of Entrepreneurial Wisdom, and PNC Financial experts will be on hand to field your questions and educate you on business financial matters.

Mrs. Marks has spent 30+ years in the Tampa Bay area honing her skill as an entrepreneur. Having owned and operated multiple businesses, including a restaurant and a multimillion dollar surgical clinic, she knows her way around business and how to operate one successfully.

Mrs. Marks states, "Owning a business takes many talents and the determination to succeed. In the course of my business operations I have experienced both the ups and the downs of the financial market. Without the knowledge of how to structure your finances to support your dreams you endanger your success. This is why I have partnered with PNC with the release of this important work."

Event date and location: October 9, 2014 between 5:30 and 6:30 pm at 2498 Gulf-to-Bay Blvd. Books available at your local bookstore and at this event.

# # #

MEDIA CONTACT: Ginger Marks, ginger.marks@documeantdesings.com 1–727–565–8500.

Braille Alphabet

Courtesy of National Braille Press Inc.

Braille Alphabet

The six dots of the braille cell are arranged and numbered:

1	4
2	5
3	6

The capital sign, dot 6, placed before a letter makes a capital letter.

1	4
2	5
3	6

The number sign, dots 3, 4, 5, 6, placed before the characters a through j, makes the numbers 1 through 0. For example: a preceded by the number sign is 1, b is 2, etc.

a	b	c	d	e	f	g	h	i	j

k	l	m	n	o	p	q	r	s	t

u	v	w	x	y	z	Capital Sign	Number Sign	Period	Comma

1	4
2	5
3	6

NATIONAL BRAILLE PRESS INC.
88 ST. STEPHEN STREET
BOSTON, MA 02115
www.nbp.org

World Braille Day Postcard

Design by DocUmeant Designs

Customize this design with your company name and colors. Be sure to change the year to fit your marketing campaign schedule. This postcard was designed using a VistaPrint Standard postcard template. If you need additional help getting your Braille Day postcard customized contact me and I'll be happy to assist you for a very nominal fee.

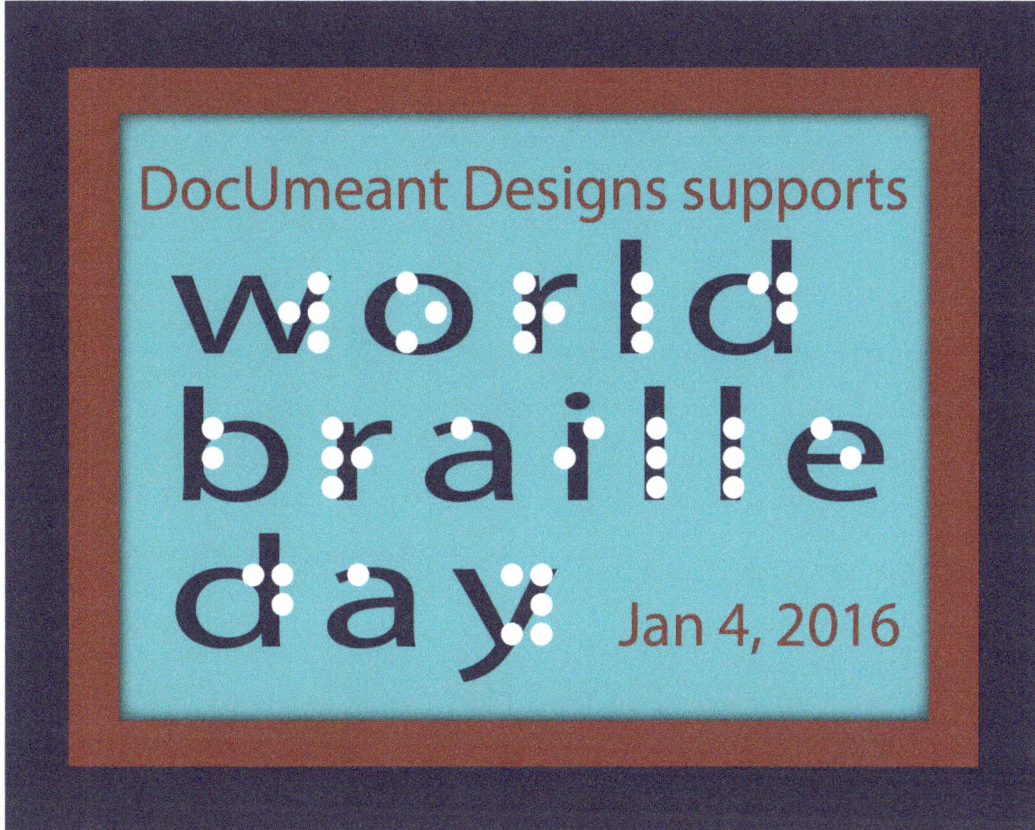

Jar of Nothing

Courtesy Craftbits.com

For this project, all you need is an empty jar, and adhesive label paper.

You can print this saying out onto some adhesive label paper suitable for your printer or print it onto normal plain paper. Use some clear craft glue to adhere it to the jar. If you want to go all out you can add some ribbon to the jar and even box it up for a great gag gift.

--- The Label ---

THE JAR OF NOTHING

Did you say nothing?

When you were asked what you wanted for

Birthday, Anniversary, Graduation, or Christmas.

Don't you remember saying NOTHING?!

Well, this time someone heard you, searched

high and low and found this perfect gift for you.

Note: These are great for Christmas fund raising stalls.

This project provided by www.craftbits.com

Womens Healthy Weight Day Chart

"Body mass index chart" by Created by User:InvictaHOG using gnuplot and Adobe Illustrator 9/23/06, released into public domain - Created by User:InvictaHOG. Licensed under Public Domain via Commons

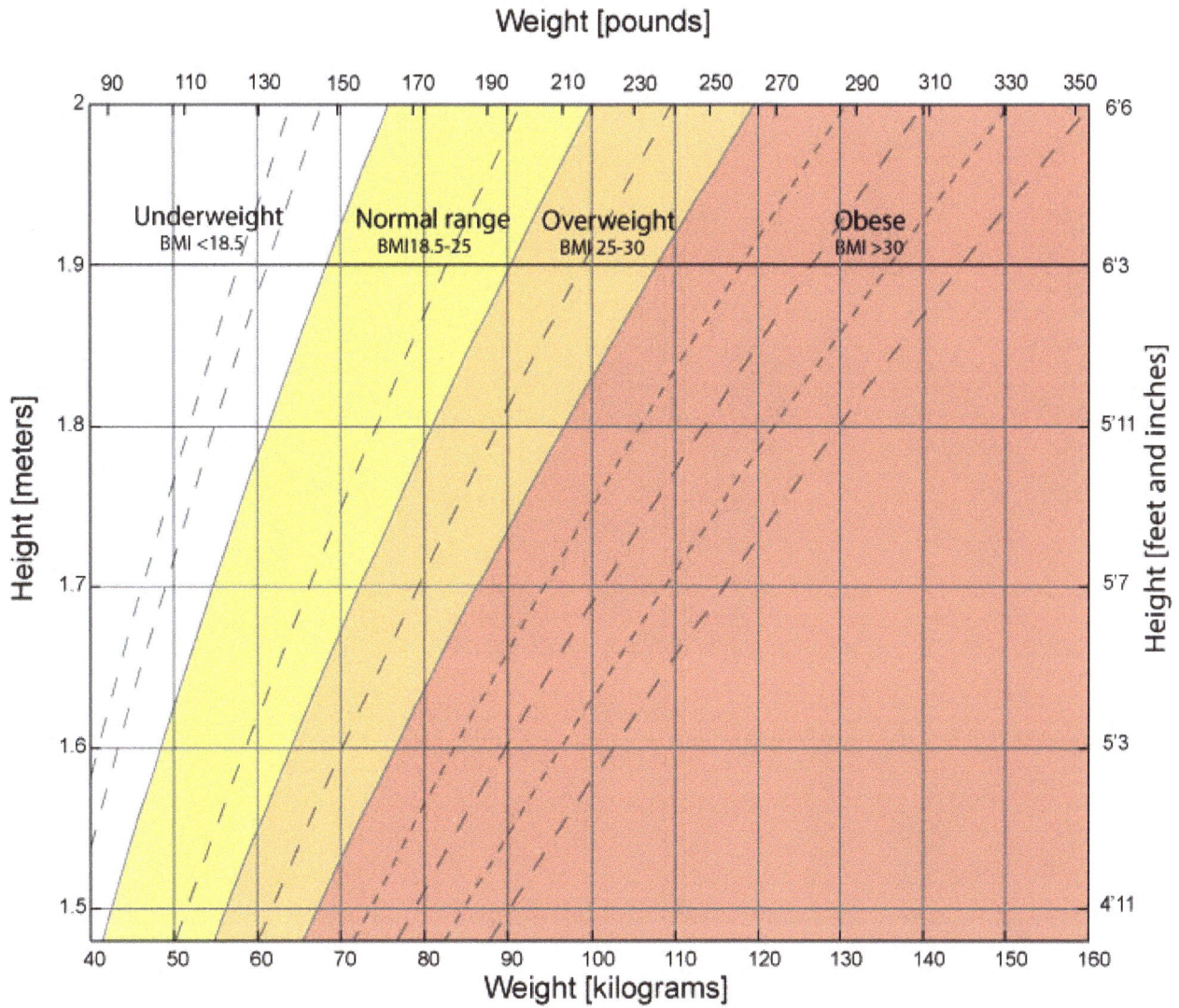

Womens Healthy Weight Day Flyer

Design by DocUmeant Designs

Take Charge!

5 keys to success

Your Business Logo

Womens Healthy Weight Day
January 23, 2016

1 KEY TIP HEADING

Tip text goes here

2 KEY TIP HEADING

Tip text goes here

3 KEY TIP HEADING

Tip text goes here

4 KEY TIP HEADING

Tip text goes here

5 KEY TIP HEADING

Tip text goes here

RECIEVE THE TOOLS, SUPPORT, AND ENCOURAGEMENT TO LOSE THE WEIGHT, AND KEEP IT OFF WHILE HAVING FUN!

BEGIN WITH THE END IN MND — IT ONLY TAKES A FEW MINUTES

Lorem Ipsum is simply dummy text of the printing and typesetting industry. Lorem Ipsum has been the industry's standard dummy text ever since the 1500s, when an unknown printer took a galley of type and scrambled it to make a type specimen book. It has survived not only five centuries, but also the leap into electronic typesetting, remaining essentially unchanged. It was popularised in the 1960s with the release of Letraset sheets containing Lorem Ipsum passages, and more recently with desktop publishing software like Aldus PageMaker including versions of Lorem Ipsum.

BEGIN WITH THE END IN MND — IT ONLY TAKES A FEW MINUTES

Lorem Ipsum is simply dummy text of the printing and typesetting industry. Lorem Ipsum has been the industry's standard dummy text ever since the 1500s, when an unknown printer took a galley of type and scrambled it to make a type specimen book. It has survived not only five centuries, but also the leap into electronic typesetting, remaining essentially unchanged. It was popularised in the 1960s with the release of Letraset sheets containing Lorem Ipsum passages, and more recently with desktop publishing software like Aldus PageMaker including versions of Lorem Ipsum.

BEGIN WITH THE END IN MND — IT ONLY TAKES A FEW MINUTES

Lorem Ipsum is simply dummy text of the printing and typesetting industry. Lorem Ipsum has been the industry's standard dummy text ever since the 1500s, when an unknown printer took a galley of type and scrambled it to make a type specimen book. It has survived not only five centuries, but also the leap into electronic typesetting, remaining essentially unchanged. It was popularised in the 1960s with the release of Letraset sheets containing Lorem Ipsum passages, and more recently with desktop publishing software like Aldus PageMaker including versions of Lorem Ipsum.

BEGIN WITH THE END IN MND — IT ONLY TAKES A FEW MINUTES

Lorem Ipsum is simply dummy text of the printing and typesetting industry. Lorem Ipsum has been the industry's standard dummy text ever since the 1500s, when an unknown printer took a galley of type and scrambled it to make a type specimen book. It has survived not only five centuries, but also the leap into electronic typesetting, remaining essentially unchanged. It was popularised in the 1960s with the release of Letraset sheets containing Lorem Ipsum passages, and more recently with desktop publishing software like Aldus PageMaker including versions of Lorem Ipsum.

YOUR BUSINESS NAME • YOUR BUSINESS URL • PHONE

Take Your Child to the Library Day Poster

Design by DocUmeant Designs

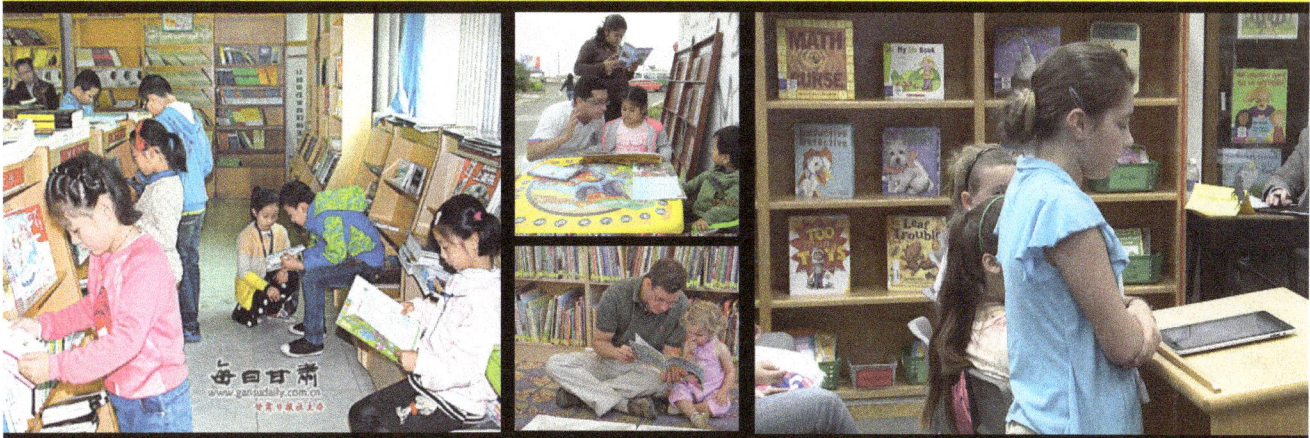

Take Your Child to the Library Day
February 6, 2016

Join us for author readings, Q&As, and more

- Helping young children build reading and language skills.
- Preparing children for success by developing early language skills.
- Motivating teens to read and discuss literature.
- Encouraging adults to experience the joy of reading.

Time:
Place:

Sponsored by DocUmeant Publishing and your local library

Free and open to the public

visit www.tycld.org for more information

Mule Day Event Poster

Design by DocUmeant Designs

Sucker Wrapper Template

Design by DocUmeant Designs

Cut along dotted line. Wrap around sucker. Tie in place with ribbon or tape.

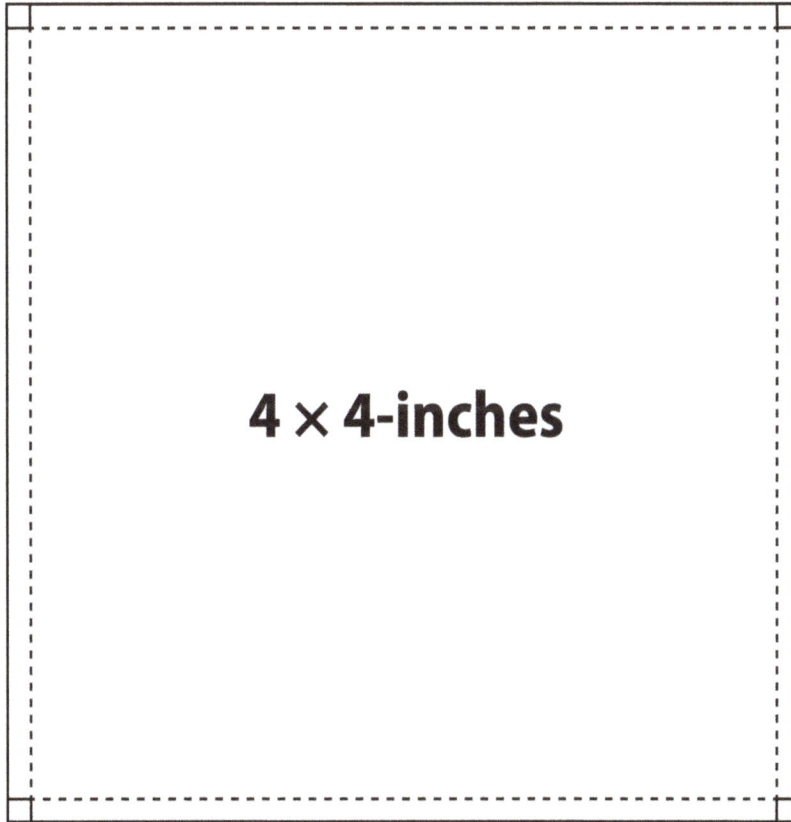

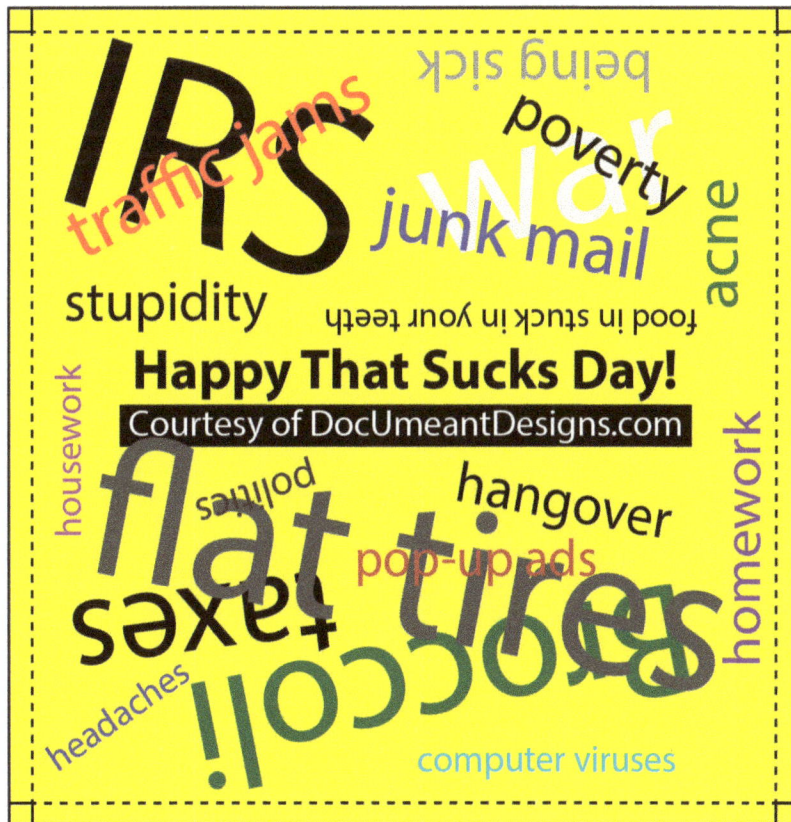

4 × 4-inches

traffic jams

IRS

being sick

poverty

war

junk mail

acne

stupidity

food in stuck in your teeth

Happy That Sucks Day!

Courtesy of DocUmeantDesigns.com

housework

flat tires

politics

hangover

homework

pop-up ads

taxes

broccoli

headaches

computer viruses

Word Games

Courtesy of Word Game World

Buzz Words

#S1   ™   by Ann Richmond Fisher

Sample and Instructions

To solve one of our exclusive Buzzword puzzles, you will use crossword-type clues, search through a honeycomb of letters, and unscramble anagrams. There's no other puzzle quite like this!

Look at this sample honeycomb. The shaded O and the six letters surrounding it spell COSTUME, which matches one of the clues below.

Try to find 7-letter words for the remaining clues. Circle the center letter of each word.
1. special set of clothes *costume*
2. soft cotton cloth _____
3. opposite of *eastern* _____
4. alike _____
5. wheeled toy with footboard _____
6. observer _____
7. ugly, terrifying creature _____

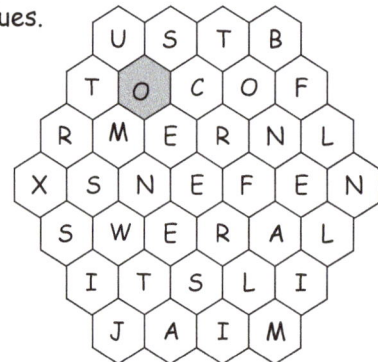

Now unscramble all 7 of the center letters to spell today's BUZZWORD.

    greeting _ _ _ _ _ _ _

Now check your answers:

2. flannel (E) 3. western (E) 4. similar (L) 5. scooter (C)
6. witness (W) 7. monster (M)

Buzzword: Unscramble all the center letters: O E E L C W M to spell WELCOME !

Word Search

Come to the Circus!

How long will it take you to find these 25 fun circus words?
The words can go across, up, down and diagonally.

B	J	R	A	E	B	V	N	R	O	C	P	O	P	W
O	E	L	C	Y	C	I	N	U	S	L	D	F	L	F
B	S	H	S	T	U	N	A	E	P	I	R	D	C	S
D	L	A	C	R	O	B	A	T	O	O	E	Q	N	I
R	R	E	Z	L	T	T	U	Q	O	N	T	S	U	A
A	E	R	A	A	I	X	N	L	H	T	S	E	K	R
P	P	E	E	C	T	O	D	J	O	A	A	S	G	K
O	O	D	Z	L	H	E	N	I	A	M	M	R	N	E
E	R	D	E	O	K	E	N	S	V	E	G	O	I	L
L	T	A	P	W	G	L	R	T	U	R	N	H	L	E
Q	H	L	A	N	T	E	N	S	M	S	I	M	G	P
A	G	I	R	S	T	I	G	E	R	U	R	F	G	H
G	I	F	T	E	M	U	T	S	O	C	S	Z	U	A
S	T	E	K	C	I	T	S	Q	L	K	I	I	J	N
G	J	U	N	O	S	R	E	C	N	A	D	Q	C	T

ACROBAT
BEAR
BLEACHERS
CLOWNS
COSTUME
DANCERS
ELEPHANT
HOOPS
HORSES

JUGGLING
LADDER
LEOPARD
LIONS
LION TAMER
MUSIC
NET
PEANUTS
POPCORN

RINGMASTER
TENT
TICKETS
TIGER
TIGHTROPE
TRAPEZE
UNICYCLE

Double Letter Animals

Double-Letter Animals

You "otter" have fun with this one!

Dive into this fun puzzle featuring animals spelled with double letters. The words can go across, up, down and diagonally, both backwards and forwards.

R	E	T	T	O	J	R	A	C	C	O	O	N	T	C	N
B	N	O	O	B	A	B	M	T	E	E	K	A	R	A	P
J	U	H	Y	L	F	R	E	T	T	U	B	G	T	R	I
R	E	L	I	V	H	L	M	O	O	S	E	Y	Y	A	Q
O	R	B	L	P	D	R	E	M	U	S	S	O	P	O	H
O	G	K	E	F	P	A	T	R	N	T	E	R	R	E	F
S	O	I	G	L	R	O	A	D	R	U	N	N	E	R	W
T	O	T	R	M	L	O	P	R	X	I	L	E	E	Z	O
E	S	T	X	U	N	E	G	O	D	R	U	B	J	E	O
R	E	E	L	O	A	W	Z	M	T	V	E	Q	J	F	D
K	A	N	G	A	R	O	O	A	T	A	A	E	S	F	P
T	I	B	B	A	R	B	G	J	G	O	M	R	D	A	E
E	K	A	N	S	E	L	T	T	A	R	R	U	K	R	C
L	L	U	G	A	E	S	H	E	E	P	S	R	S	I	K
V	T	C	A	R	O	T	A	G	I	L	L	A	A	G	E
L	L	A	M	A	L	L	I	R	O	G	Y	D	A	P	R

AARDVARK	GOOSE	PARROT
ALLIGATOR	GORILLA	RABBIT
BABOON	HIPPOPOTAMUS	RACCOON
BULLFROG	KANGAROO	RATTLESNAKE
BUTTERFLY	KITTEN	ROADRUNNER
DEER	LLAMA	ROOSTER
EEL	MOOSE	SEA GULL
FERRET	OPOSSUM	SHEEP
GAZELLE	OTTER	SQUIRREL
GIRAFFE	PARAKEET	WOODPECKER

Anagram

International Anagrams

In keeping with our theme of word games for people around the world, here's a set of International Anagrams!

Find the name of a **country** and its **capital** for each item.

Example: RAN IN HEART = Tehran, Iran

1. SPAM DID RAIN

2. RIVET IN A SAUNA

3. GRAY COP TIE

4. HUG FAT SILK BANANA

5. MORE LAITY

6. RAP CAR FINES

7. DUAL LINEN BIRD

8. THANK KING BOA, LAD!

9. ROW YON, ALSO

For the answers, look at the next page.

Answers:
1. Madrid, Spain
2. Vienna, Austria
3. Cairo, Egypt
4. Kabul, Afghanistan
5. Rome, Italy
6. Paris, France
7. Dublin, Ireland
8. Bangkok, Thailand
9. Oslo, Norway

World Turtle Day Flyer

Design by DocUmeant Designs

FUN TURTLE FACTS

- Turtles are reptiles.
- Turtles have a hard shell that protects them like a shield, this upper shell is called a 'carapace'.
- Turtles also have a lower shell called a 'plastron'.
- Not all turtles can hide their heads inside their shells when attacked by predators.
- Turtles have existed for around 215 million years.
- Turtles are cold blooded.
- The largest turtle is the leatherback sea turtle, it can weigh over 2000 lb!
- Turtles lay eggs.
- In some species of turtle the temperature determines if the egg will develop into a male or female, lower temperatures lead to a male while higher temperatures lead to a female.
- Some turtles lay eggs in the sand and leave them to hatch on their own. The young turtles make their way to the top of the sand and scramble to the water while trying to avoid predators.
- Sea turtles have special glands which help remove salt from the water they drink.
- Many turtle species are endangered.

DocUmeant Designs • www.DocUmeantDesigns.com

Image courtesy of logoopenstock.com

Soul Food Month Event Flyer

Design by DocUmeant Designs

Bloomsday Postcard

Design by DocUmeant Designs from book cover.

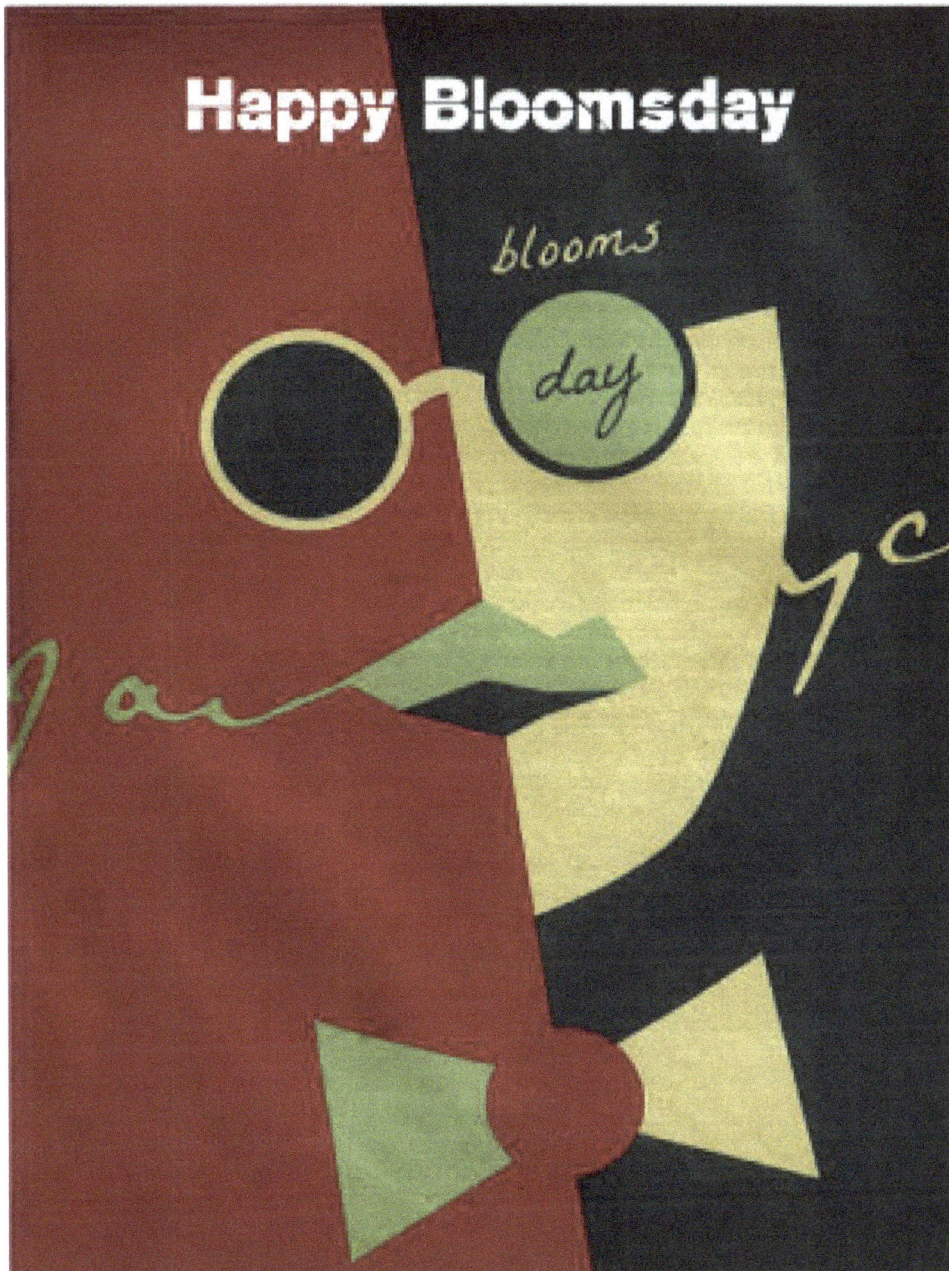

4 Tips for Ensuring a Successful Take Your Dog To Work Day® at Your Company

Courtesy of Pet Sitters International

The 17th annual celebration of PSI's Take Your Dog To Work Day (TYDTWDay®) is on Friday, June 24, 2016 and many businesses—even those not traditionally pet friendly—are opening their doors to employees' dogs for this special day.

Whether your businesses has never allowed dogs in the workplace before or your company is dog friendly year round, it's important to review your TYDTWDay policies to ensure your celebration will be a successful one.

Event creator Pet Sitters International (PSI) offers these tips for participating dog owners to help ensure management, employees and pets are all comfortable on TYDTWDay:

1. Dogs should be kept on a leash, unless in the employee's office or cubicle. Even the best-behaved dogs may not understand that not everyone loves puppy kisses or a pouncing pooch. Respect co-worker's space by keeping your dog leashed when outside of your office or cubicle. Co-workers who want to pet your dog will likely come to you.

2. Employees should use a baby gate to prevent dogs from leaving their office unsupervised. In the middle of an important sales call or during a visit from a business partner is not the best time for Fido to dash out of your office. Give your dog space to roam in your office while avoiding an unplanned escape by using a baby gate.

3. Specific areas, such as bathrooms or employee dining halls, should be designated as dog-free. Even on TYDTWDay, there will be limitations to where your dog can roam. Work with management and co-workers to decide which areas of the office will be dog-free.

4. Have a back-up plan for taking the dog home if he is not comfortable in the work environment. While most dogs love spending a day at the office, it may be that your dog is not ready to enter the workforce. Have a back-up plan, such as a spouse, friend or professional pet sitter who can take care of your pet if he needs to leave the office.

Created by PSI in 1995, TYDTWDay encourages employers to experience the joys of pets in the workplace for one special day to celebrate the great companions dogs make and promote adoptions from local shelters, rescue groups and humane societies.

Businesses and pet owners interested in learning more about TYDTWDay are encouraged to download a free action pack at Takeyourdog.com. To locate a professional pet sitter in your area to assist with a TYDTWDay event, visit PSI's Official Pet Sitter Locator at http://www.petsit.com/locate.

Gruntled Worker Sticker

Design by DocUmeant Designs

Use Avery Round Sticker Labels. Then download their template for Word and place one in each blank label template space. Now print them up and hand them out to show your fellow workers or people you meet today how 'gruntled' you truly are.

Gruntled Worker Breakroom Poster

Design by DocUmeant Designs

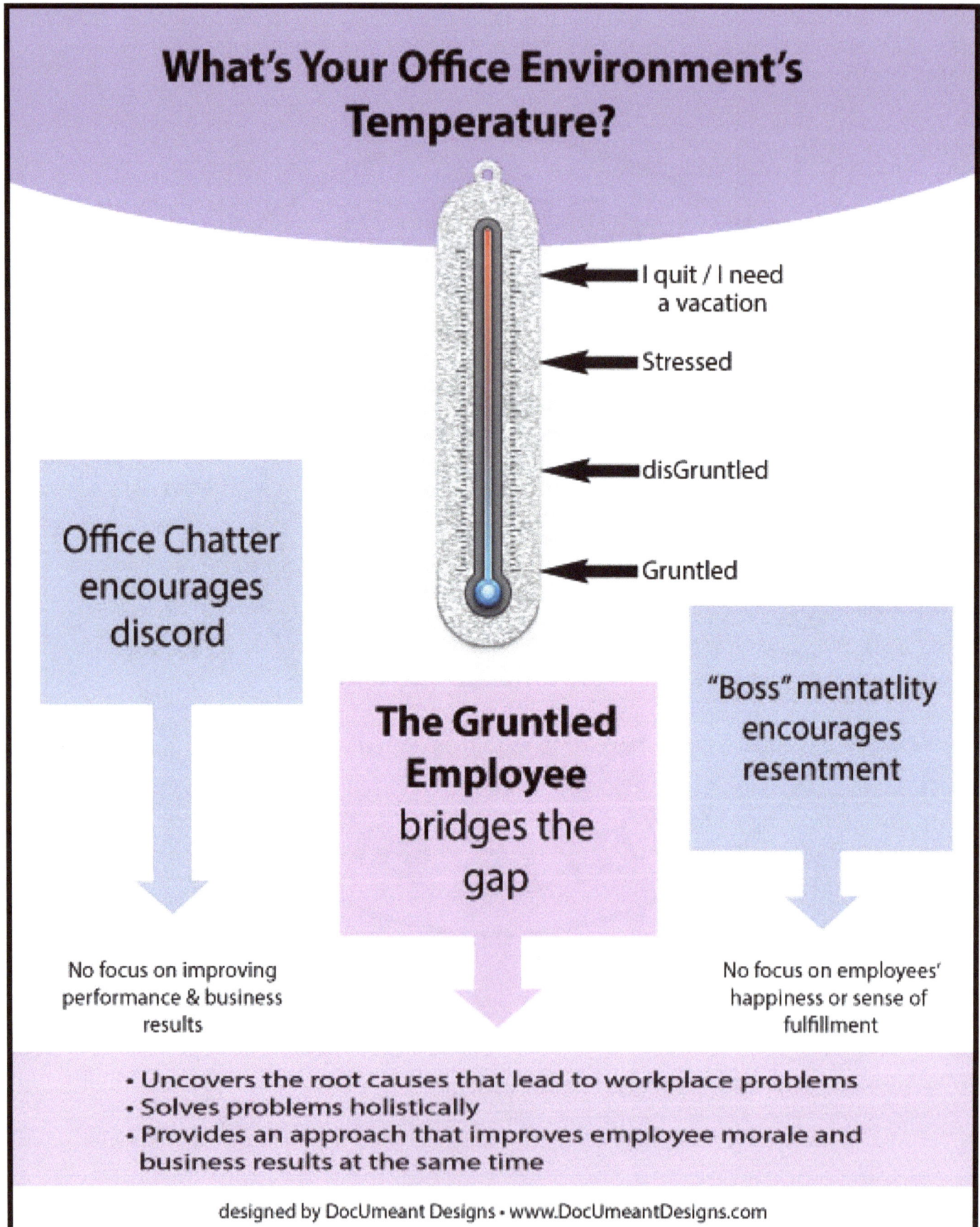

What's Your Office Environment's Temperature?

← I quit / I need a vacation

← Stressed

← disGruntled

← Gruntled

Office Chatter encourages discord

The Gruntled Employee bridges the gap

"Boss" mentatlity encourages resentment

No focus on improving performance & business results

No focus on employees' happiness or sense of fulfillment

- Uncovers the root causes that lead to workplace problems
- Solves problems holistically
- Provides an approach that improves employee morale and business results at the same time

designed by DocUmeant Designs • www.DocUmeantDesigns.com

National Lighthouse Day Poster

Designed by DocUmeant Designs

Virtual Food Drive

Courtesy of North Texas Food Bank

Holding a Virtual Food Drive provides an easy, immediate and effective way for you or your group to get involved with ending hunger. The benefits of hosting an on-line drive include:

- Virtual format makes it easy to use and manage.

- It allows for 100 percent group involvement.

- It's eco-friendly and cost-efficient.

- Every $1 provides three meals.

- Dividing your group into competing teams adds fun and boosts morale.

No shopping, no lifting, no driving, and best of all, no lines! Donating through a Virtual Food Drive is cost effective, efficient, and couldn't be easier.

Simply click on the food items you wish to donate and then click Check Out once you have reached your desired contribution amount.

If you would like to talk to someone regarding your Virtual Food Drive, please contact Jessica Quinonez at JessicaQ@ntfb.org or 214-270-2054.

- See more at: http://web.ntfb.org/get-involved/donate-food/virtual-food-drive#sthash.nL4XBmI2.dpuf

There are several Virtual Hosts for your Virtual Food Drive with some listed in the Resources. I am told that you will see a 60% increase in funds with this new and simple to use tool.

Tarzan Day Fact Questions

1. Who is the author of the Tarzan books? (Edgar Rice Burroughs)

2. How old was Tarzan when he was orphaned in the jungle? (He was just an infant)

3. When was the first Tarzan story published? (Oct 1912)

4. What was the name of the story? (Tarzan of the Apes, a Romance of the Jungle)

5. What actor first played Tarzan? (Johnny Weissmuller)

6. Name the six media types that Tarzan appeared in. (Comic books, comic strips, TV, movies, books, and radio)

7. What is Tarzan's English name? (John Clayton, Viscount Graystoke)

8. What is Tarzan's ape tribe called? (Mangani)

9. Who was Tarzan's love interest? (Jane Porter)

10. What ability is Tarzan most noted for? (Swinging on a vine)

Extra Credit

11. Can you name all the other actors who portrayed Tarzan? (Elmo Lincoln, Lex Barker, Buster Crabbe, Jock Mahoney, Herman Brix, Frank Merrill, Ron Ely, Mike Henry, Christopher Lambert, Gordon Scott, Joe Lara, Wolf Larson, Harrison Chad, Casper Van Dien, Tony Goldwyn, Denny Miller, Travis Fimmel, Kellan Lutz, Alexander Skarsgård, Alex D Linz, Anton Zetterholm, Craig Garner)

Backpack Awareness Day Samples

Courtesy of The American Occupational Therapy Association, Inc.

Poster

Backpack Facts: What's All the Flap About?

National School Backpack Awareness Day is an annual event held on the third Wednesday of every September. Across the country, backpack events educate parents, students, educators and school administrators, and communities about the serious health effects that backpacks that are too heavy or worn improperly have on children. Backpack Day is also a time to promote the full range of occupational therapy benefits and services

- More than 79 million students in the United States carry school backpacks.[1]
- More than 2,000 backpack-related injuries were treated at hospital emergency rooms, doctor's offices, and clinics in 2007.[2]
- It is recommended that a loaded backpack should never weight more than 10% of the student's total body weight (for a student weighing 100 pounds, this means that the backpack should weight no more than 10 pounds).[3]
- About 55% of students carry a backpack that is heavier than the recommended guideline of 10% of the student's total body weight.[4]
- In one study with American students ages 11 to 15 years, 64% reported back pain related to heavy backpacks. Twenty one percent reported the pain lasting more than 6 months.[5]
- In a study on the effect of backpack education on student behavior and health, nearly 8 out of 10 middle school students who changed how they loaded and wore their backpacks reported less pain and strain in their backs, necks, and shoulders.[6]
- According to a study by Boston University, approximately 85% of university students self-report a discomfort and pain associated with backpack usage.[7]
- The way backpacks are worn affects your health. The height of the backpack should extend from approximately 2 inches below the shoulder blades to waist level or slightly above the waist. It is recommended that individuals always wear the backpack on both shoulders so the weight is evenly distributed.[8]

Sources

1. American Community Survey. *2007 American Community Survey 1-Year Estimates* [Data file]. Retrieved May 14, 2009, from http://factfinder.census.gov/servlet/DTTable?_bm=y&-geo_id=01000US&-ds_name=ACS_2007_1YR_G00_&-SubjectID=15258038&-_lang=en&-mt_name=ACS_2007_1YR_G2000_B14001&-format=&-CONTEXT=dt
2. U.S. Consumer Product Safety Commission National Electronic Injury Surveillance System (NEISS) Database (2007). Numbers quoted are the estimated figures.
3. Hu, J., Jacobs, K., & Pencina, M. (Submitted for publication). Backpack usage and self-reported musculoskeletal discomfort in university students.
4. Graduate Program in Physical Therapy, Simmons College. (2001, February 12). *Children's Backpacks Are Too Heavy, New Study Shows* [Press Release]. Retrieved May 14, 2009, from http://www.simmmons.edu/shs/about/news/pt/2003/back.shtml
5. UC Newsroom, University of California. (2004, August 26). *Back to school; heavy packs endanger kids' health, study shows* [Press Release]. Retrieved May 14, 2009, from http://www.universityofcalifornia.edu/news/article/6575
6. Feingold, A. J., & Jacobs, K. The effect of education on backpack wearing and posture in a middle school population. *Work,* 18, 287–294.
7. Hu, J., Jacobs, K., & Pencina, M. (Submitted for publication). Backpack usage and self-reported musculoskeletal discomfort in university students.
8. Berghaus, R. (2008, August). Take a load off. *BU Today.* Retrieved May 14, 2009, from http://www.bu.edu/today/2008/09/16/take-load

AOTA® The American Occupational Therapy Association, Inc.

OT Rex Backpack Coloring Page

COLOR ME!

OT Rex Junior knows how to pack his backpack light and wear it right! In recognition of AOTA's National School Backpack Awareness Day, give OT Rex Junior some color to get him ready for a great day at school!

SCHOOL

AOTA® The American Occupational Therapy Association, Inc.

Tips on Purchasing a Backpack

TIPS FOR PURCHASING A BACKPACK

The American Occupational Therapy Association (AOTA) urges parents and caregivers to consider the following when selecting a backpack this school year:

APPROPRIATE SIZE. Make sure the height of the backpack extends from approximately 2 inches below the shoulder blades to waist level, or slightly above the waist.

SHOULDERS. Backpacks should have well-padded shoulder straps that can be worn on both shoulders so when packed with books, the weight can be evenly balanced by the student.

HIP BELT. Backpacks with a hip or chest belt take some strain off sensitive neck and shoulder muscles and improve the student's balance.

FIT. Just as your child will try on clothes and shoes when back-to-school shopping, experts say it is important to try on backpacks, too.

FROM THE EXPERT. "A child wearing a backpack incorrectly or that is too heavy can be contributing risk factors for discomfort, fatigue, muscle soreness, and musculoskeletal pain especially in the lower back," says Karen Jacobs, EdD, OTR/L, CPE, clinical professor of occupational therapy at Boston University, and an expert on school ergonomics and healthy growth and development of school-age children.

National School Backpack Awareness Day

Pack It Light,
Wear It Right

American Occupational Therapy Association

Find backpack safety tips at www.aota.org/backpack

My Backpack Weigh Sheet

My backpack weighs:

My bag should weigh less than 10% of my body weight. My bag is:

☐ too heavy   ☐ just right

AOTA's National School **Backpack Awareness Day**
Pack it light, wear it right!

AOTA®
The American Occupational Therapy Association, Inc.

Find backpack safety tips at: aota.org/backpack

Backpack Weigh Sheet

Weigh-In Sheet

AOTA's National School Backpack Awareness Day

If your school is interested in how many students have heavy backpacks, use this sheet to collect information.

Grade	Age	Backpack Weight	Student Weight
		pounds	pounds
		pounds	pounds
		pounds	pounds
		pounds	pounds
		pounds	pounds
		pounds	pounds
		pounds	pounds
		pounds	pounds
		pounds	pounds
		pounds	pounds
		pounds	pounds
		pounds	pounds
		pounds	pounds
		pounds	pounds

National School Backpack Awareness Day

pack it light, wear it right

Grade _____ Age _____

Backpack Weight _____ pounds

Student Weight _____ pounds

My backpack is _____% of my body weight.

National School Backpack Awareness Day

pack it light, wear it right

Grade _____ Age _____

Backpack Weight _____ pounds

Student Weight _____ pounds

My backpack is _____% of my body weight.

National School Backpack Awareness Day

pack it light, wear it right

Grade _____ Age _____

Backpack Weight _____ pounds

Student Weight _____ pounds

My backpack is _____% of my body weight.

National School Backpack Awareness Day

pack it light, wear it right

Grade _____ Age _____

Backpack Weight _____ pounds

Student Weight _____ pounds

My backpack is _____% of my body weight.

Corny Facts

Courtesy of Popcorn.org

- Americans consume some 16 billion quarts of this whole grain, good-for-you treat. That's 54 quarts per man, woman, and child.

- Compared to most snack foods, popcorn is low in calories. Air-popped popcorn has only 31 calories per cup. Oil-popped is only 55 per cup.

- Popcorn is a type of maize (or corn), a member of the grass family, and is scientifically known as Zea mays everta.

- Of the 6 types of maize/corn—pod, sweet, flour, dent, flint, and popcorn—only popcorn pops.

- Popcorn is a whole grain. It is made up of three components: the germ, endosperm, and pericarp (also known as the hull).

- Popcorn needs between 13.5-14% moisture to pop.

- Popcorn differs from other types of maize/corn in that is has a thicker pericarp/hull. The hull allows pressure from the heated water to build and eventually bursts open. The inside starch becomes gelatinous while being heated; when the hull bursts, the gelatinized starch spills out and cools, giving it its familiar popcorn shape.

- Most U.S. popcorn is grown in the Midwest, primarily in Indiana, Nebraska, Ohio, Illinois, Iowa, Kentucky and Missouri.

- Many people believe the acres of corn they see in the Midwest during growing season could be picked and eaten for dinner, or dried and popped. In fact, those acres are typically field corn, which is used largely for livestock feed, and differs from both sweet corn and popcorn.

- The peak period for popcorn sales for home consumption is in the fall.

- Most popcorn comes in two basic shapes when it's popped: snowflake and mushroom. Snowflake is used in movie theaters and ballparks because it looks and pops bigger. Mushroom is used for candy confections because it doesn't crumble.

- Popping popcorn is one of the number one uses for microwave ovens. Most microwave ovens have a "popcorn" control button.

- "Popability" is popcorn lingo that refers to the percentage of kernels that pop.

- There is no such thing as "hull-less" popcorn. All popcorn needs a hull in order to pop. Some varieties of popcorn have been bred so the hull shatters upon popping, making it appear to be hull-less.

- How high popcorn kernels can pop? Up to 3 feet in the air.

- On September 29, 2006 a new record was set for the World's Largest Popcorn Ball, as measured by the Guinness Book of World Records. Eight feet in diameter and nearly 24.5 feet in circumference, this gargantuan confectionary creation weighed in at a whopping 3,423 pounds. It took two days for employees of The Popcorn Factory to create the ball.

- If you made a trail of popcorn from New York City to Los Angeles, you would need more than 352,028,160 popped kernels!

A History of Popcorn Poppin'

Popcorn is one of the oldest American foods and has had a significant role in our history. Some of the oldest ears of popcorn were found in 1948 by archaeologists exploring the Bat Cave in west central New Mexico. These ears were proven to be about 4,000 years old.

In South America, kernels of popcorn found in burial grounds in the coastal deserts of North Chile were so well preserved they would still pop even though they were 1,000 years old!

Popcorn was used by the Native Americans as a staple in their diet and for decoration. Sixteenth century Aztec Indians used popcorn in their ceremonies; young women danced a "popcorn dance" and wore garlands of popcorn in their hair.

Popcorn was probably NOT served at the first Thanksgiving. There is no indication that popcorn had made its way East at the time of the earliest settlers.

Early Native Americans threw kernels directly into the fire or into heated sand. Once popped, the corn was sifted and then pounded into a fine, powdery meal and later mixed with water for eating. This was especially handy when traveling, making it a true American "to go" meal.

By the 1840s popping corn had become a popular recreational activity.

Colonists mixed ground popcorn with milk and ate it as a breakfast food. Popcorn pudding—made from ground popcorn—was lauded by the likes of Ella Kellogg, Fannie Merritt Farmer and Mary Hamilton Talbott. And shortly after the end of World War II, a shortage of baking flours forced bread makers to substitute up to 25% of wheat flour with ground popped popcorn.

By the 1870s popcorn was a common item sold in grocery stores, and at concession stands at circuses, carnivals, and street fairs.

Charles Cretors, founder of C. Cretors and Company, Chicago, introduced the world's first mobile popcorn machine at the World's Columbian Exposition in Chicago in 1893. Scientific American reported: "This machine....was designed with the idea of moving it about to any location where the operator would be likely to do a good business. The apparatus, which is light and strong, and weighing but 400 or 500 pounds, can be drawn readily by a boy or by a small pony to any picnic ground, fair, political rally, etc., and to many other places where a good business could be done for a day or two."

During the Depression, popcorn sold for 5 or 10 cents a bag and was considered an affordable luxury for struggling families.

During World War II, sugar was sent overseas for U.S. troops, which meant there wasn't much sugar left in the states to make candy. Thanks to this unusual situation, Americans ate three times as much popcorn as usual.

In 1945, an engineer named Percy Spencer accidentally discovered that microwave radio signals could be used to cook foods. His experiments with popcorn led, in part, to the development of the microwave oven.

Perfect Popcorn Poppin' Tips

Popping Tips for Good Old-Fashioned Popcorn

Nothing's better than a great batch of popcorn. Here are a few tips for perfect popping, every time.

Warm the heavy pan or heavy skillet. Be sure the lid of the pan is loose enough to allow steam to escape and keep the pan moving when popping popcorn on the stove.

Add ¼ cup of vegetable (cooking) oil to the pan. Allow the oil to heat. The best popping temperature is between 400-460 degrees Fahrenheit. Note: Oil burns at 500 degrees Fahrenheit, so if your oil starts to smoke, it's too hot.

Test the heat of the oil by dropping in one or two kernels. When the kernel spins in the oil you're ready to add the remaining popcorn. Pour just enough kernels to cover the bottom of the pan.

Cover and shake the pan to be certain the oil coats each kernel. When you hear the last few pops, remove the pan from the heat, take off the lid and empty the popped popcorn into a large bowl.

Simply Perfect Popcorn Ideas

Popcorn Fixin's

Looking to spice up your popcorn? Here are a few topping favorites:

- Garlic salt
- Parmesan cheese
- Thyme
- Cumin
- Oregano
- Dry taco seasoning mix
- Dry ranch-style seasoning mix
- Lemon pepper
- Italian herbs: oregano, basil, marjoram, thyme, and crushed rosemary.
- French herbs: marjoram, thyme, summer savory, basil, rosemary, sage, and fennel
- Cinnamon, brown sugar, nutmeg

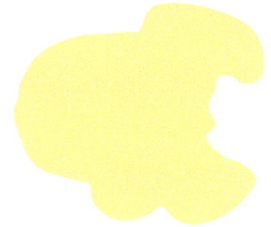

There are countless tasty treats you can make using popcorn. Be creative and have fun. For more scrumptious snacking ideas, visit us on the Web at www.popcorn.org.

Popcorn Poppin' Month Recipes

Maple Pumpkin Spice Popcorn

2 tablespoons brown sugar

2 tablespoons maple syrup

1 1/2 teaspoons pumpkin spice mix

1 tablespoon butter or margarine

1/2 cup chopped pecans, optional

5 cups popped popcorn

In a large saucepan or pot, heat brown sugar, maple syrup and pumpkin pie spice mix over medium heat. Cook, stirring, 3 minutes or until sugar is dissolved and mixture is bubbling. Stir in butter until melted and well blended. Add pecans, if desired, and popcorn and stir until well coated.

Allow mixture to cool before serving. Serve immediately or store in an airtight container.

Yield: 5 cups

Crispy Crunchy Apple Popcorn

6 cups popped popcorn

1 tablespoon butter, melted

2 teaspoons sugar

1/2 teaspoon cinnamon

2 cups dried apple chips

Preheat oven to 300° F. Line a 9 x 13-inch baking pan with foil; butter foil. Spread popcorn in pan and drizzle with melted butter; toss popcorn.

Sprinkle popcorn with sugar and cinnamon and toss again. Heat in oven 7 minutes. Sprinkle apple chips over popcorn and heat an additional 3 minutes. Serve warm or cool to room temperature. Store in an airtight container.

Yield: 7 cups

Popcorn Caramel Apples

1 quart popped popcorn

1 (9.5 oz.) package caramels, unwrapped (35 caramels)

¼ cup light cream or 'half and half'

4 lollipop sticks (or wooden candy apple sticks)

4 apples

½ cup chocolate chips

Sugar sprinkles

Decorative ribbon, optional

Place popcorn in a large bowl; set aside. Place a sheet of waxed paper on work surface.

Heat caramels and cream in a small sauce pan over medium-low heat. Stir frequently until caramels are melted and cream is blended into caramels.

Push a stick into an apple center and dip into caramel. Spoon caramel over apple to coat completely. Place caramel–coated apple into bowl of popcorn and press popcorn onto caramel to cover completely. Place apple on waxed paper to set; repeat with remaining apples.

Place chocolate chips in a small, resealable plastic bag. Microwave 10 seconds and press chips to aid melting. Repeat, heating at 10-second intervals, until chips are completely melted. Cut a small corner off bag and squeeze chocolate onto each apple allowing chocolate to drip down sides. Sprinkle with sugar sprinkles.

Tie a bow to each apple stick, if desired. To serve, cut apple into slices.

Yield: 4

Pop-a-rific Popcorn Balls
3 quarts popped popcorn

1 (1-lb.) pkg. marshmallows

1/4 cup (1/2 stick) butter or margarine

Place popped popcorn in a large bowl. Set Aside. In large saucepan, heat marshmallows and butter or margarine over low heat until melted and smooth. Pour over popcorn, tossing gently to mix well. Cool to allow handling (5 min.). Butter hands well and form 2 ½-inch balls.*

Yield: About 14 balls

Happy Halloween Mini Popcorn Balls
10 cups popped popcorn

1 (1-lb.) pkg. miniature marshmallows

1/4 cup (1/2 stick) butter or margarine

1 cup diced dried fruit (papaya, mango or peaches)

1 cup butterscotch chips

Orange food coloring (optional)

Mix popcorn, fruit and butterscotch chips in large bowl; set aside. In large saucepan, heat marshmallows and butter over low heat until melted and smooth. Stir in several drops of food coloring if desired. Pour over popcorn and candy, tossing to coat evenly. Cool to allow handling (5 min.). Butter hands well and form into 3-inch balls.

Yield: About 16 balls

Chili Lime Popcorn
1 quart popped popcorn

1 teaspoon brewer's yeast powder (or nutritional yeast; available in health food stores)

1 teaspoon lime juice

1/2 teaspoon chili powder

1/4 teaspoon salt

Preheat oven to 300° F. Spread popcorn on a baking sheet. Sprinkle yeast powder, lime juice, chili powder and salt over popcorn. Heat about 7 minutes and toss just before serving. Serve warm. Makes: 1 quart

Popcorn S'mores

1 cup firmly packed light brown sugar

1/2 cup (1 stick) butter or margarine

1/2 cup corn syrup

1/2 teaspoon baking soda

10 cups freshly popped popcorn

1 package (10 1/2 oz.) miniature marshmallows

2 cups mini graham cookies (teddy bears)

1 cup chocolate chips

Combine brown sugar, butter and corn syrup in medium saucepan. Cook over high heat for 5 minutes; remove from heat and stir in baking soda.

Combine popcorn and marshmallows in large bowl. Pour sugar mixture over popcorn to coat. Gently stir in graham cookies and chocolate chips. Spread mixture evenly into greased 15 x 10 inch pan. Let cool completely. Break into pieces. Store in an airtight container.

Yield: 20 pieces

Spicy Cajun Popcorn & Nuts

8 cups popped popcorn

1/2 cup toasted, coarsely chopped pecans

1/2 cup peanuts

1/4 cup (1/2 stick) butter or margarine, melted

1/4 teaspoon each: dry mustard, garlic powder

1/8 teaspoon cayenne pepper

Place popcorn and nuts in large bowl.

In small microwave-safe bowl, microwave butter on HIGH until melted, about 30 seconds. Stir in dry mustard, garlic powder and cayenne pepper.

Drizzle over popcorn mixture and toss well.

Yield: 9 servings

For more delicious recipes, visit them on the Web at www.popcorn.org.

Popcorn Month Infographic

Designed by DocUmeant Designs

Contact me to customize this with your data and organization at designer@documeantdesigns.com.

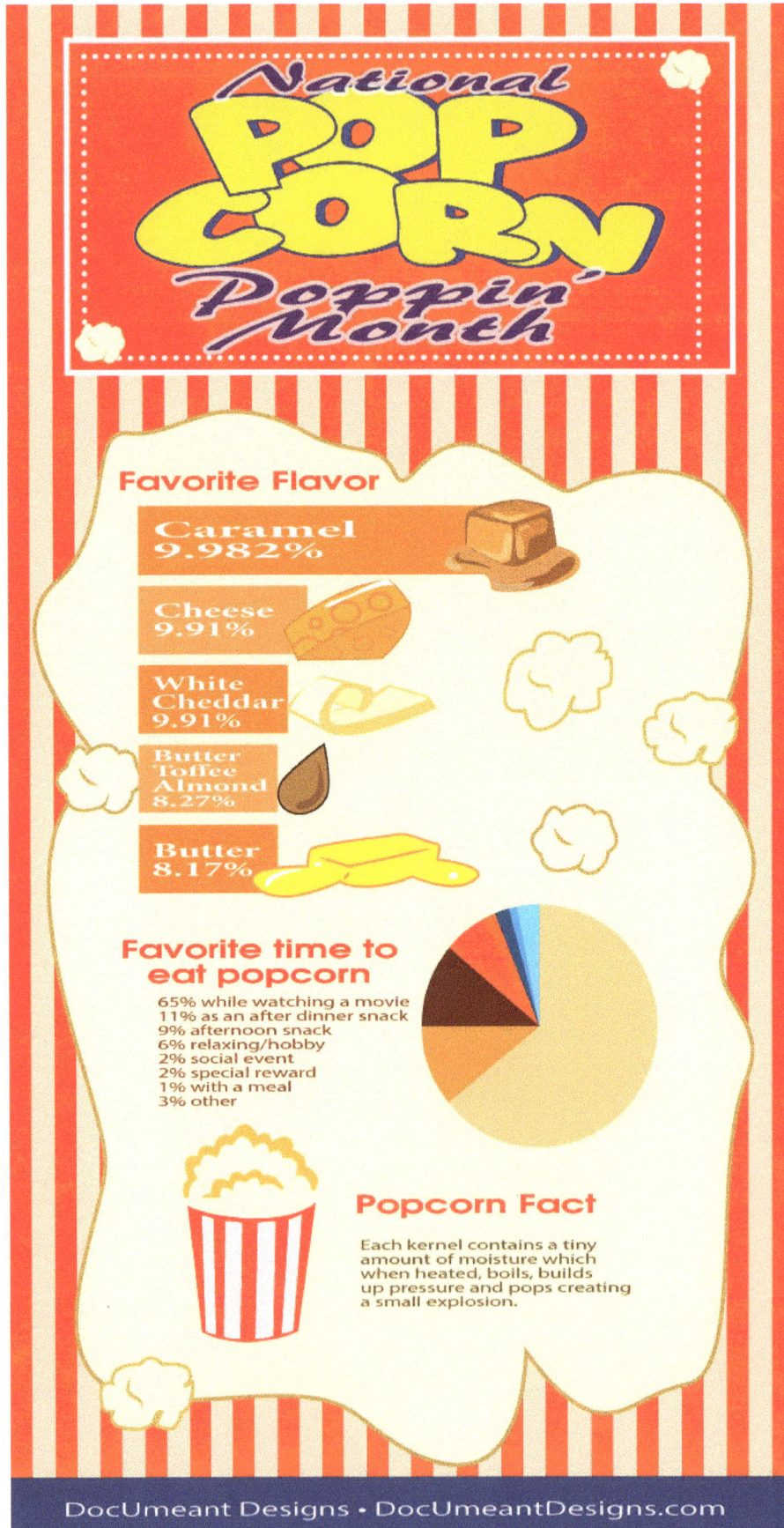

National POP CORN Poppin' Month

Favorite Flavor

Caramel
9.982%

Cheese
9.91%

White
Cheddar
9.91%

Butter
Toffee
Almond
8.27%

Butter
8.17%

Favorite time to eat popcorn

65% while watching a movie
11% as an after dinner snack
9% afternoon snack
6% relaxing/hobby
2% social event
2% special reward
1% with a meal
3% other

Popcorn Fact

Each kernel contains a tiny amount of moisture which when heated, boils, builds up pressure and pops creating a small explosion.

DocUmeant Designs • DocUmeantDesigns.com

Guardian Angel Postcard

Design by DocUmeant Designs

Guardian Angel Card Sayings

This is your Guardian Angel saying ...

Even if things seem a little bit crazy where you are right now, from up here you look pretty good. That tangled mess that's got you worried, it's just a dark cloud ... but there's a rainbow on the other side.

Sometimes life sends us a small miracle in the form of a person we almost mistake for an angel ... and all we can do is say, "Thanks" ... Thanks for being my angel.

Dick Tracy Day Poster

Design by DocUmeant Designs

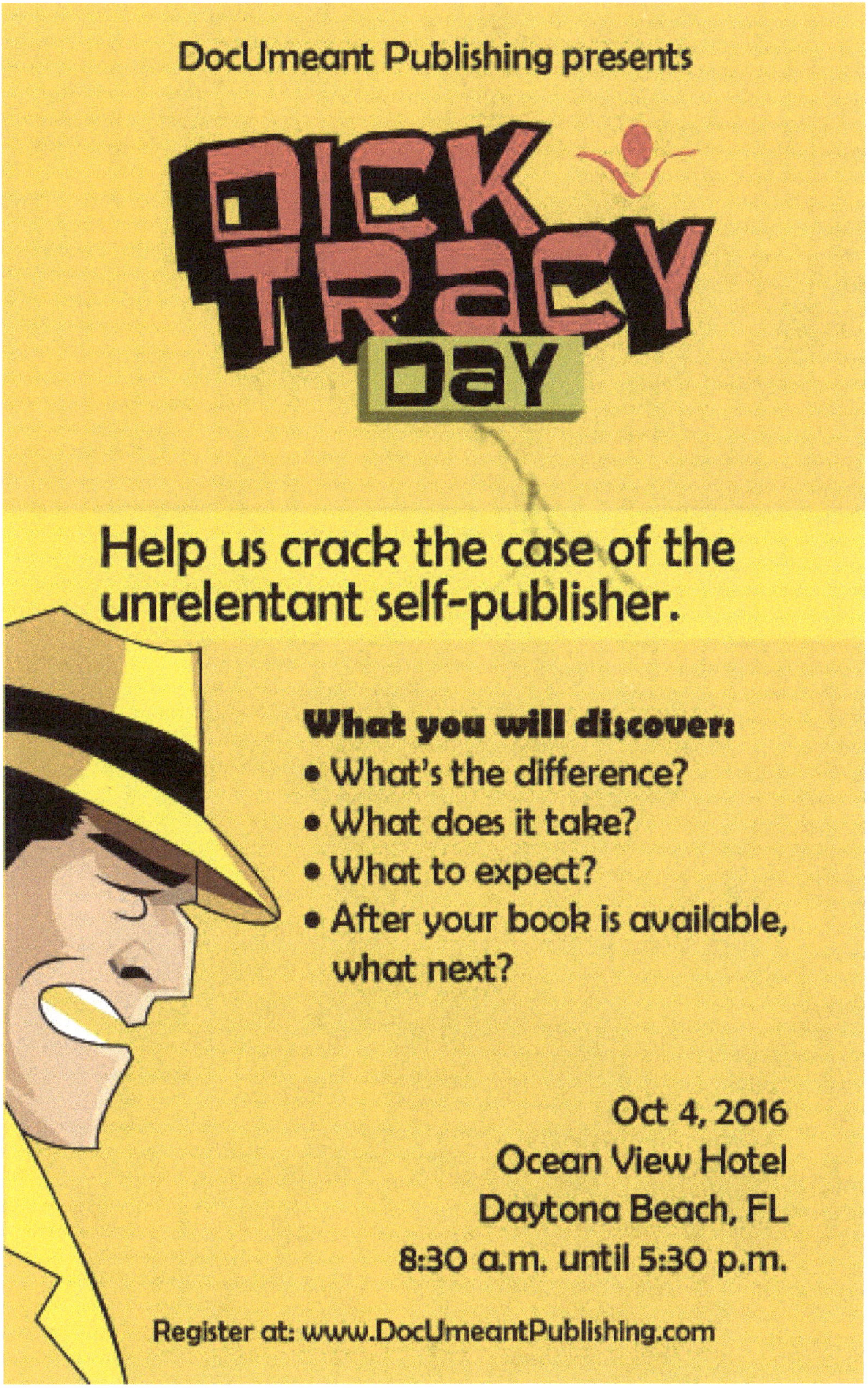

Hagfish Day Slime

Courtesy of WhaleTimes.org

What you'll need:

1 Tsp Metamucil

1 cup boiling water

Whisk Metamucil into boiling water. Keep at a gentle rolling boil. Stir constantly. Cook about 5 to 7 minutes. The mixture will change from a syrupy to a gooey, gelatin mixture. The mixture should be pliable but not too thin or thick. Remove from heat and allow to cool at least 45 to 60 minutes. Store in resealable bags.

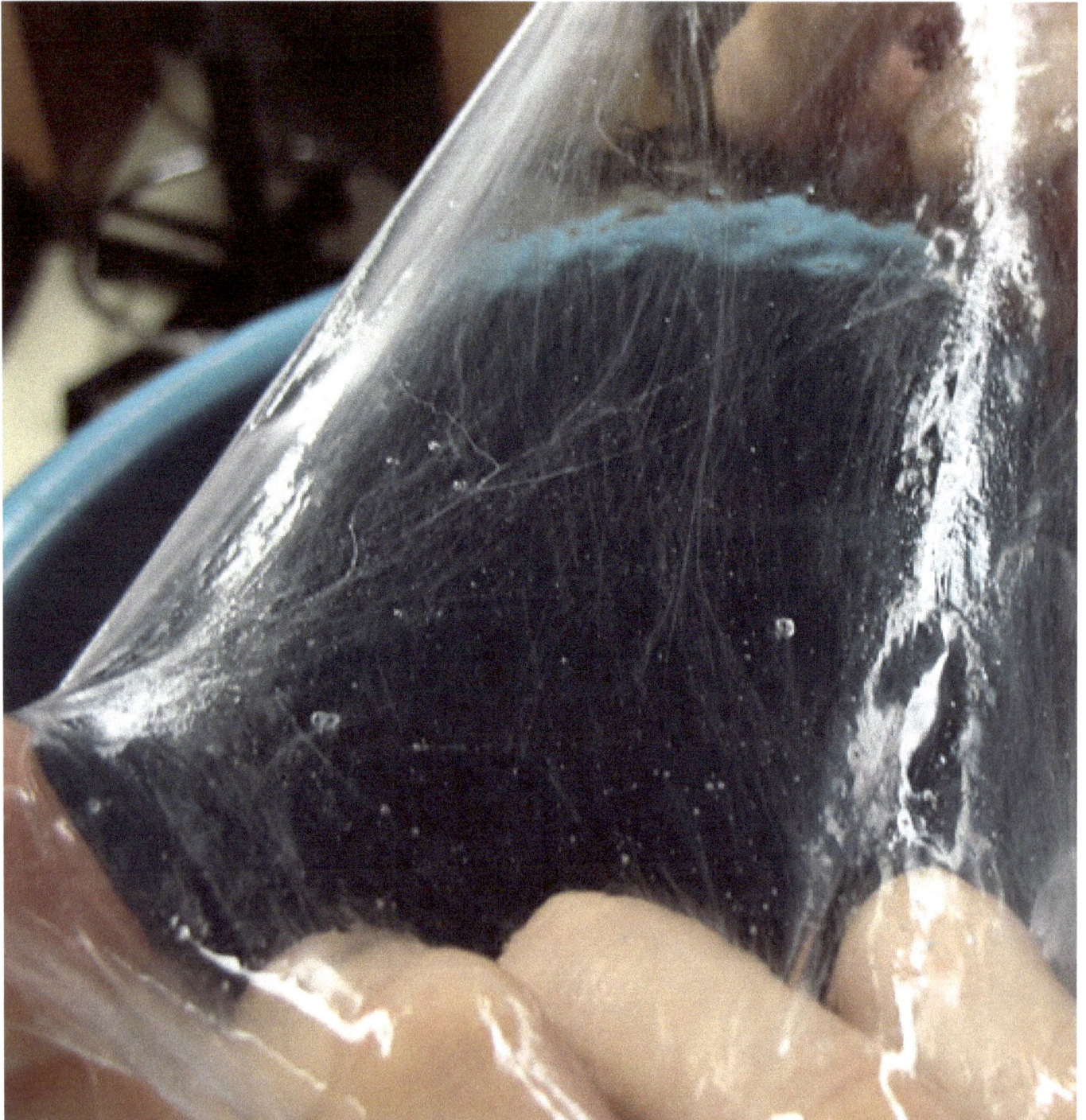

Hockey Day Event Poster

Design by DocUmeant Designs

Cookie Recipes

Snickerdoodles

1 1/2 cups sugar

1/2 cup butter or margarine, softened

1/2 cup shortening

2 eggs

2 3/4 cups Gold Medal™ all-purpose or unbleached flour

2 teaspoons cream of tartar

1 teaspoon baking soda

1/4 teaspoon salt

1/4 cup sugar

2 teaspoons ground cinnamon

DIRECTIONS:

Heat oven to 400 degrees.

Mix 1 1/2 cups sugar, the butter, shortening and eggs in large bowl. Stir in flour, cream of tartar, baking soda and salt.

Shape dough into 1 1/4-inch balls. Mix 1/4 cup sugar and the cinnamon. Roll balls in cinnamon-sugar mixture. Place 2 inches apart on ungreased cookie sheet.

Bake 8 to 10 minutes or until set. Remove from cookie sheet to wire rack.

NOTE: Add 1 cup chopped Snickers™ candy bars for a chunky, chewy twist on this favorite recipe.

Ranger Cookies

1/2 cup shortening

1/2 cup white sugar

1/2 cup packed brown sugar

1 egg

1/2 teaspoon vanilla extract

1 cup all-purpose flour

1/2 teaspoon baking soda

1/4 teaspoon baking powder

1/4 teaspoon salt

1 cup rolled oats

1 cup whole wheat flake cereal

1/2 cup flaked coconut

Photo By MS. B

DIRECTIONS:

Cream shortening with sugars. Beat in egg and vanilla.

Mix together dry ingredients and stir into wet mix. Place by heaping spoonfuls on an ungreased baking sheet.

Bake at 375 degrees F (190 degrees C) for 10 minutes. Remove immediately to cool.

Butter Pecan Turtle Cookies

1-3/4 cups flour

1 cup brown sugar

1/2 cup butter, melted

2 cups whole pecan halves

2/3 cup butter (no substitutes)

1/2 cup brown sugar

2 cups milk chocolate chips

DIRECTIONS:

Preheat oven to 350 degrees. Combine ingredients until the mixture looks like cornmeal. Pat evenly into a 13" x 9" baking pan.

Sprinkle pecans over crust. In a small saucepan, combine butter and brown sugar.

Cook over medium heat, stirring constantly, until mixture boils for 1 minute and looks syrupy. Drizzle over the pecans. Make sure that when you're drizzling the brown sugar syrup over the crust that you keep the layer thin and even. Bake bars at 350 degrees 17-22 minutes until bubbly over entire surface. Remove from oven.

Sprinkle immediately with milk chocolate chips, let melt for a few minutes, then swirl a knife through some of the chips to marble. Don't try to spread the chips over the whole pan. 36 bars

Christmas Delight Cookies

This is a secret family recipe. Don't tell anyone. ;)

1/2 cup butter

1 pkg. (3 oz.) cream cheese

3/4 cup sugar (separate out 1 tsp)

1 egg yolk

1 tsp vanilla

2 cups sifted all purpose flour

1/2 tsp baking powder

1/4 tsp salt

1 cup finely chopped walnuts

DIRECTIONS:

Mix butter, cream cheese, and 1 tsp sugar by hand (do not use a blender).

Beat together egg yolk and vanilla. Add to cream cheese mixture.

In a separate bowl combine flour, baking powder, salt, and remaining sugar.

Gradually add flour mixture to cream cheese mixture.

Add chopped walnuts.

Preheat oven to 350 degrees. Bake 10 minutes or until brown on bottom.

***Note:** When doubling this recipe do not double the flour. Use only 3 1/2 to 3 3/4 cups flour; 4 cups is too much!

Santa's Whiskers

1 cup butter, softened

1 cup sugar

2 Tbsp milk

1 tsp vanilla or rum flavoring

2 1/2 cups all-purpose flour

3/4 cup finely chopped red or green candied cherries

1/2 cup finely chopped pecans

3/4 cup flaked coconut

Courtesy of Brenda @ mealplanningmagic.com

DIRECTIONS:

In mixing bowl cream together butter and sugar.

Blend in milk and vanilla or rum flavoring.

Stir in flour, chopped candied cherries, and chopped pecans.

Form dough into two 8-inch rolls. Roll in flaked coconut to coat outside. Wrap in waxed paper or clear plastic wrap; chill thoroughly.

Cut into 1/4-inch slices. Place on ungreased cookie sheet.

Bake at 375 degrees til edges are golden, about 12 minutes.

Makes about 60.

Now for a couple of not so much as cookies, but still favorite recipes.

Seven Layer Cookie Bars

1 stick butter or margarine

1-1/2 cups Graham cracker crumbs

1 can condensed milk

6 oz. pkg. chocolate chips

6 oz. pkg butterscotch chips

1 can coconut

1 cup chopped nuts (I prefer pecans, but walnuts are a healthier and less expensive alternative)

DIRECTIONS:

Melt margarine in 9 x 13-inch pan.

Pat down graham cracker crumbs into margarine.

Pour condensed milk over that and then layer the rest of the ingredients.

Bake at 350 degrees for 25 minutes.

Cool and refrigerate before cutting into squares.

White Chocolate Krispies aka Angel Poo
Prep Time: 10 mins
Total Time: 15 mins
Servings: 20

1 lb white chocolate

1 cup Cap'n Crunch peanut butter crunch cereal

1 cup Rice Krispies

3/4 cup dry roasted salted peanut

3/4 cup roasted salted cashews

1 cup white miniature marshmallow

DIRECTIONS:

Line a large sheet pan with wax paper; set aside. Cut white chocolate into small chunks, add to a medium pot and cook over medium-low heat, stirring constantly, until completely melted and smooth, 2-3 minutes.

Remove pot from heat, add Cap'N Crunch, Rice Krispies, peanuts, and cashews and stir gently to coat. Set aside to let cool slightly for 2–3 minutes, then stir in marshmallows.

Drop mounds of the chocolate mixture (about 3 tablespoons each) onto the prepared pan, keeping them spaced about 1" apart, to make 3-inch wide candies. Set aside in a cool spot until completely set. Serve immediately, or store in an airtight container in a cool spot for up to one week.

Cream Cheese Mints

Freeze in layers of wax paper in an airtight container.
Prep: 1 hour, 10 minutes
Stand: 4 hours

1 (8oz.) pkg. cream cheese

¾ c. butter, softened

2-lbs. powdered sugar

½ tsp. peppermint extract

6 drops red liquid food coloring (optional)

DIRECTIONS:

Powdered sugar

Cook cream cheese and butter in a saucepan over low heat, stirring constantly, until smooth. Gradually stir in powdered sugar; stir in peppermint extract.

Divide cream cheese mixture into 2 portions, if desired. Stir 2 drops coloring into 1 portion and remaining 4 drops coloring into second portion.

Shape each portion of mixture into 1-inch balls. Dip a 2-inch round cookie stamp or bottom of a glass into powdered sugar.

Press each ball to flatten. Let stand, uncovered, 4 hours or until firm. Freeze if desired. Yields: 8 dozen.

7 Things About Artificial Hearts That You Should Know

Courtesy of SynCardia

From 1969 to September 5, 2014, 1,413 artificial hearts of 13 different designs have been implanted in heart failure patients. Here's an update on the state of this life-saving technology.

1. Growing Demand for Artificial Hearts

According to the U.S. Department of Health & Human Services, about 4,000 people wait for a donor heart transplant on any given day, while the supply of approximately 2,300 donor hearts annually has been flat in the U.S. for over 20 years.

Among European Union countries, 3,400 patients were on waiting lists for a donor heart in 2012. According to the European Commission's Department of Health and Consumers, only 2,004 transplants were conducted that year.

2. The Most Used Artificial Heart

There have been 1,413 implants of all artificial heart designs from 1969 to September. 5, 2014. The SynCardia temporary Total Artificial Heart and its direct predecessors account for 1,352 or 96% of all implants. Of that number, nearly 500 SynCardia Hearts have been implanted since 2010.

An artificial heart must fit in the patient's chest without causing complications. Recent artificial heart designs are significantly heavier and larger than an adult human heart, which averages between 250 and 350 grams. For example, the AbioCor replacement heart ($250,000) weighs 1,090 grams and the Carmat artificial heart ($181,000-$233,000) weighs 900 grams. Only large adult patients can accommodate artificial hearts of that size.

The SynCardia Heart ($124,800, plus Freedom driver service charges) weighs 160 grams, less than half the weight of a human heart, and is similar in size to an average human heart, which makes more patients eligible for implantation.

3. Duration of Support for Patients on Artificial Hearts

Artificial hearts help patients survive and regain their health for transplant. The shortage of donor hearts causes patients to wait longer for heart transplants.

The patient who has been supported the longest was Italian patient Pietro Zorzetto, who had a SynCardia Total Artificial Heart for nearly four years—1,374 days—prior to his successful heart transplant September 11, 2011.

One-third of current SynCardia Artificial Heart patients have been supported for more than a year, including some who have worn the device for two years or more (47% outside of the United States, 21% in the U.S.).

4. Improved Quality of Life

As of September 5, 2014, French resident Frédéric Thiollet, 37, has been living with his SynCardia Total Artificial Heart for 1,122 days. For three years, he has been on the 13.5-pound Freedom® portable driver, which powers the device and is FDA, Health Canada and CE approved. He has lived at home and in his community waiting for a matching donor heart since his discharge from the Thorax Institute at University Hospital of Nantes December 15, 2011.

"I have recuperated all my physical functions," says Thiollet. "I have enjoyed an effective resurrection, a new birth. Physically I have no limit. I am as strong and powerful as before, even more so than before."

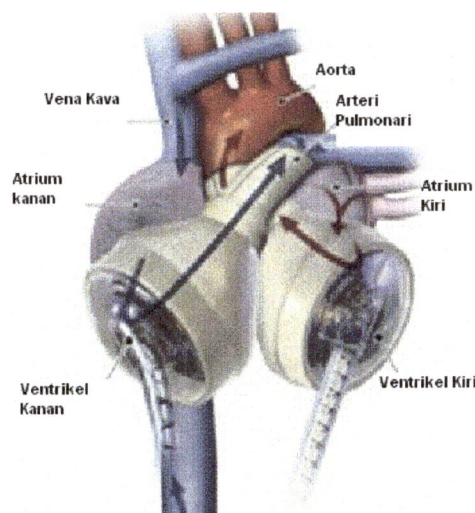

By Orensanquiks (Own work) [CC BY-SA 3.0 (http://creativecommons.org/licenses/by-sa/3.0) or GFDL (http://www.gnu.org/copyleft/fdl.html)], via Wikimedia Commons

With the Freedom portable driver, SynCardia Total Artificial Heart patients resume their lives with nearly unlimited mobility.

Christopher Larsen boxes to stay in shape.

Chris Marshall hiked a total of 607 miles before receiving his heart transplant.

Randy Shepherd completed the 4.2-mile Pat's Run event.

Lexi Henderson, at age 16 years, was the youngest person to be discharged from the hospital with the Freedom portable driver and has since received a donor heart.

5. Highest Bridge to Transplant Rate

According to data published in the 2004 New England Journal of Medicine from the 10-year pivotal clinical study which led to FDA approval, 79% of patients who received a CardioWest, an earlier design of the SynCardia Total Artificial Heart, were bridged to transplant.

This is the highest bridge to transplant rate for any approved artificial heart or ventricular assist device in the world.

From June 23, 2006 to September 30, 2012, 82% of patients who had lived one year with a SynCardia Total Artificial Heart implant either received a donor heart transplant (70.3%) or were alive and waiting for a matching donor heart (11.6%), according to the third-quarter 2012 INTERMACS report.

6. Reliability Statistics

Because of the small implantation numbers of nearly all of the artificial heart designs, it is impossible to establish credible data on the reliability of those designs.

The one exception is the SynCardia Total Artificial Heart. It and its predecessors have been implanted 1,352 times over more than 30 years. In those three decades of use

The valves in the Total Artificial Heart have never failed. (after the first implant)

The diaphragm, which is responsible for pumping blood in and out of each ventricle, has a reliability rate exceeding 99.5% for more than 1,350 implants representing 2,700+ diaphragms.

7. Status of 2 Regulatory-Approved Devices and 1 Design Under Study

Only two artificial heart designs are FDA approved: the SynCardia Total Artificial Heart and the AbioCor replacement heart.

The AbioCor replacement heart was implanted 15 times; the last implant was in 2009.

That same year, the Boston Globe published a November 23 story about Abiomed, manufacturer of AbioCor. In the article, Abiomed chief executive Michael Minogue was quoted as saying he considers the self-contained artificial heart "the sports car you watch on television, but you can't buy from your dealer . . . It's a unique product."

On December 18, 2013, the first implant of the Carmat bioprosthetic heart, which is similar in design to the AbioCor, was conducted under a clinical feasibility study. The patient died after 74 days. A March 16, 2014 article by the Reuters news service said, "The device's inventor, French surgeon Alain Carpentier, told the weekly Journal du Dimanche…that the heart had stopped after a short circuit, although the exact reasons behind the death were still unknown."

On September 8, 2014 Reuters issued a story that quoted the French health ministry confirming that a second Carmat artificial heart implant was conducted on August 5 at Nantes, the same hospital where Thiollet received his SynCardia Total Artificial Heart.

SynCardia Systems, Inc., manufacturer of the SynCardia Total Artificial Heart, is working with U.S., Canadian and European regulatory agencies. In the U.S., SynCardia is working with the FDA to launch clinical trials this year into using the smaller, 50cc version of the current 70cc Total Artificial Heart and a separate study for permanent use (destination therapy). The 50cc heart is designed to be used for patients of smaller stature including women, smaller men and many pediatric patients. If approved, the 50cc and the approved 70cc SynCardia Total Artificial Hearts are designed to fit all adults and many pediatric patients.

Like SynCardia on Facebook

Follow SynCardia on Twitter @SynCardia

Connect with SynCardia on LinkedIn

Share and Discover on Google+

###

Media Contact:

Don Isaacs

Vice President of Communications

SynCardia Systems, Inc.

Cell: (520) 955-0660

Appendix B: LINKS

Link Checker

For Chrome: https://chrome.google.com/webstore/detail/check-my-links/ojkcdipcgfaekbeaelaapakgnjflf-glf?hl=en-GB (I know this is out of alpha order, but a good link deserves top billing, don't you think? ;)

Article Marketing Sites

http://goarticles.com/

http://internationalpractice.com/business/

http://thephantomwriters.com/index.php

http://www.article99.com

http://www.articledashboard.com/

http://www.articlegarden.com/

http://www.articlesbase.com/

http://www.articleson.com/

http://www.biz–whiz.com

http://www.dropjack.com/

http://www.selfgrowth.com

http://www.ideamarketers.com/

http://www.information–exchange.net/

http://www.isnare.com

http://www.ladypens.com/

http://www.promotionworld.com

http://wahm–articles.com

http://www.wahsolutionsmagazine.com/

http://www.writeandpublishyourbook.com/magazine/

https://contributor.yahoo.com/signup.shtml

http://www.ezinearticles.com

Auto Responder Services

AWeber: www.aweber.com/

Constant Contact: www.constantcontact.com/

Your Mailing List Provider: www.yourmailinglistprovider.com/

Books & Movies

99 Things You Wish You Knew Before Your Identity Was Stolen: http://www.amazon.com/dp/0983212295

99 Things You Wish You Knew Before Your Mobile Device Was Hacked: http://www.amazon.com/dp/1937801195

A Natural History of the Senses by Diane Ackerman: http://www.amazon.com/dp/0679735666/

Bowdler's Shakespeare: http://www.amazon.com/dp/0923891951

Celebrate the Senses by Eric Rolls: http://www.amazon.com/gp/product/0170062880

Madly In Love With Me by Christine Arylo: http://madlyinlovewithme.com/books/#booktrailer

Max & Myron Books by Wendy VanHatten: http://www.amazon.com/s/ref=nb_sb_noss?url=search-alias%3D-stripbooks&field-keywords=Max+and+Myron%2C+VanHatten&rh=n%3A283155%2Ck%3AMax+and+Myron\c+VanHatten

Complete Library of Entrepreneurial Wisdom: http://www.CLEWbook.com

Operation North Pole Days: http://youtu.be/27l63MY3H_A

Presentational Skills for the Next Generation: http://www.amazon.com/dp/B005EA01QO

Take Me Out of the Bathtub: http://books.simonandschuster.com/9780689829031

The Better Hour: The Legacy of William Wilberforce: http://www.thebetterhour.org/tbh/index.htm

Greeting Card Companies

123Greetings: http://www.123greetings.com

American Greetings: http://www.americangreetings.com/

Blue Mountain: www.bluemountain.com/

Cyberkisses: http://www.cyberkisses.com/

Day Springs: www.dayspring.com/ecards/

eGreetings: http://www1.egreetings.com/

Evite: www.evite.com

Grab Cart: http://www.grabcart.com/product/awauthentic-105500?gclid=Cj0KEQiA7tCjBRDulMny5rfM0dk-BEiQA7fcshbjuryi4LmLFbaFDI3nLn64-sADRa556aI33wUbOUIAaAo6M8P8HAQ —Civil War cards

Hallmark: http://www.hallmark.com/

Jacquie Lawson: www.jacquielawson.com/

Operation Write Home: http://operationwritehome.org/

Punchbowl Greetings: http://www.punchbowl.com/invitations/preview/5400a4b424e4b36a3e000029/5400a56bb f947f655a000111

Send Out Cards: www.sendoutcards.com/

Podcast Directories

Corante-Podcasting: http://podcasting.corante.com/—Weblog with news and events related to podcasting.

Hipcast: http://www.hipcaStcom/—Audio and video podcasting service. Includes news and on-line tour.

iTunes: http://blog.lextext.com/blog/_archives/2005/1/4/225172.html—The iTunes Store puts thousands of free podcasts at your fingertips.

Lextext.com: How to Podcast RIAA Music Under License—http://blog.lextext.com/blog/_ archives/2005/1/4/225172.html—Discussion of legal ways to podcast music. [Podcast is 5.3 MB in size]

The Liberated Syndication Network: http://www.libsyn.com/—Full featured service tailored specifically for media Self-publishing and podcasting. Price is based on usage, changing monthly if needed.

NPR: http://www.npr.org/rss/podcast/podcast_directory.php—Over 50 public radio stations and producers are working with NPR to bring you podcasting.

The Podcast Directory: http://www.podcastdirectory.com/—Up to date and relevant podcast directory. Podcasting News: http://www.podcastingnews.com/—Information relating to podcasting, a podcast directory, and a user forum.

SkypeCasters: http://www.henshall.com/blog/archives/001056.html—Introducing instructions for SkypeCasting, the solution for podcasters to create audio recordings from interviews and conference calls using Skype.

Skype Forums: http://forum.skype.com/viewtopic.php?t=12788—Recording a Skype Conversation–Discussion thread covering software, techniques, and legal tidbits.

Wikipedia: Podcast –http://en.wikipedia.org/wiki/Podcast—Encyclopedia entry covering basics of the topic.

Promotional Product Supply Companies

4imprint: https://www.4imprint.com/ —offers free samples

Build A Sign: http://www.buildasign.com/

CafePress: www.cafepress.com/

Crown Awards: https://www.crownawards.com/

iPrint: http://www.iprint.com

Judie Glenn Inc: www.judieglenninc.com—ask for Tracey Arehart

Northwest Territorial Mint: http://custom.nwtmint.com/

Overnight Prints: http://www.overnightprints.com/

Promotional Products: www.promotionalproducts.org/—Get free quotes from multiple vendors

Staples: www.StaplesPromotionalProducts.com

VistaPrint: www.Vistaprint.com

World Class Medals : http://www.worldclassmedals.com/

Zazzle: http://www.zazzle.com/custom/buttons

Quote Sources

Bartleby: http://www.bartleby.com/

Brainy Quote: http://www.brainyquote.com/quotes/keywords/resources.html

Leadership Now: http://www.leadershipnow.com/quotes.html

Quote Garden: http://www.quotegarden.com/index.html

Quoteland: http://www.quoteland.com/

The Quotations Page: http://www.quotationspage.com/

Think Exit: http://thinkexist.com/quotes/american_proverb/

Woopidoo!: http://www.woopidoo.com/

Singing Telegram Services

Aarons Singing Telegrams: http://www.SingingTelegramsLosAngeles.com

American Singing Telegrams: http://www.americansingingtelegrams.com/

Gig Masters Singing Telegrams: http://www.gigmasters.com/SingingTelegram/Singing-Telegram.htm

Happy Entertainment Party Productions: http://www.happyentertainment.com/

The International Singing Telegram Company: http://balloonstunesworldwide.com/

Orange Peel Moses: http://www.customsingingtelegrams.com/

PreppyGrams Singing Telegrams: http://www.preppygrams.com/specialdelivery.html

Sunshine Singing Telegram Service: http://www.sunshinesingingtelegrams.com

The International Singing Telegram Company Inc.: https://www.facebook.com/pages/The-International-Singing-Telegram-Company-Inc/173670102142

Wacky Jack's Singing Telegrams & Balloons: http://www.wackyjacktelegrams.com/

Teleconference Companies

What is: www.business.com/directory/telecommunications/business_solutions/conferencing/ Buyer's Guide: www.buyerzone.com/telecom_services/telecon_services/buyers_guide5.html Free Conference: www.freecon-ference.com/

Teleconference Live: http://teleconference.liveoffice.com

Teleconferencing Services: www.teleconferencingservices.net/

Wholesale Conference Call: www.wholesaleconferencecall.com/

Yugma Desktop Sharing Software: http://vur.me/gmarks/Yugma

Virtual Assistant Companies

A Clayton's Secretary (Kathie M Thomas): http://vadirectory.net/

Administrative Services (Gazelle Simmons): http://www.admnsrvcs.com/

Collins Administrative Services (Tracy Collins): http://www.collins–admin.com

Key Business Partners, LLC (Teresa Morrow): http://www.keybusinesspartners.com/ —Specializes in On-line Book Promotion for Authors

MJ Stern, VA: http://www.mjstern–va.com/ —Specializes in Internet marketing

My Efficient Assistant (Sandy Parker): www.MyEfficientAssistant.com

RJ Professional Services (Rebekah Zobel Jones—Specializes in Real Estate): http://rjprofessionalservices.com/

Streamline Your Marketing (Crystal Pina): http://www.streamlineyourmarketing.com

Virtual Freedom 4 You (Corrie Petersen): http://virtualfreedom4you.com/

Virtual Sun (Lynne Cutler): http://www.virtualsunsupport.com/

Writer's 1 Stop (Luanne Stevenson): http://writers1stop.com/

Webinar Services

Adobe Acrobat Connect Pro: http://tryit.adobe.com/us/connectpro/universalvoice/?sdid=DNOSU

BrainShark: http://brainshark.com/

Cisco WebEx: http://webex.com/

ClickWebinar: http://www.clickwebinar.com/

DimDim: http://www.dimdim.com/

Elluminate: http://www.elluminate.com/Products/?id=3

Freebinar: http://www.freebinar.com/

Free Conference Calling: http://www.freeconferencecalling.com/

Fuze: http://www.fuzemeeting.com/

GatherPlace: http://www.gatherplace.net/start/

Google+ Hangouts: https://plus.google.com/hangouts

GoToMeeting: http://www.gotomeeting.com/fec/

GoToWebinar: http://www.gotomeeting.com/fec/webinar

IBM Lotus Unyte: https://www.unyte.net/

iLinc: http://www.ilinc.com/

Infinite Conference: http://www.infiniteconference.com/

InstantPresenter: http://www.instantpresenter.com/

Intercall: http://www.intercall.com/smb/

Mega Meeting: http://www.megameeting.com/professional.html

Microsoft Office Live Meeting: http://www.microsoft.com/on-line/officE-livE-meeting/buy.mspx

Nefsis: http://www.nefsis.com/

Peter Pan Birthday Club: http://www.sjbhealth.org/body_foundation.cfm?id=1875

PGi Better Meetings: http://www.pgibettermeetings.com/

ReadyTalk: http://www.readytalk.com/

Saba Centra: http://saba.com/

StageToWeb: http://www.stagetoweb.com/livE-event–webcasting.html

STREAM57: http://www.stream57.com/

Tokbox: http://tokbox.com/

Video Seminar Live: http://www.videoseminarlive.com/

Yugma: https://www.yugma.com/

Zoho: http://www.zoho.com/meeting/

Appendix C: RESOURCES

American Occupational Therapy Association, Inc., National School Backpack Awareness Day: http://www.aota.org/Conference-Events/Backpack-Safety-Awareness-Day/Handouts.aspx

Blood Donor Drive Info: www.givelife.org or call 1-800-GIVE-LIFE (1-800-448-3543)

Craftbits—http://www.Craftbits.com

English Heritage—http://www.english-heritage.org.uk/visit/kidstakeover/be-a-king-or-queen-for-the-day/

Feeding America: http://www.feedingamerica.org/ways-to-give/set-the-table/

Foodlebrites, Favorite Food puns: http://foodlebrities.com/post/101983379/pete-townshend-pea

Fun Trivia, Facts about Tarzan: http://www.funtrivia.com/en/Movies/Tarzan-7847.html

GW Little, Dog Costumes: http://www.gwlittle.com/product/Dog_Turkey_Costume/dog_animal_costumes

Habitat for Humanity: http://www.habitat.org/

Homemade Pie Capital of Minnesota—Braham Pie Day, PO Box 383, Braham, NM 55006; Phone: 320-296-4956; www.pieday.com

Joe Miller's Jests—https://archive.org/details/joemillerscomple00mill

Karen Mullarky, "No Mullarkey" Personal Training, LLC: www.KarenMullarkey.com

King Turkey Day Official Website: http://www.kingturkeyday.net

Made by Meg Too, Argyle Business Card Holder: https://www.etsy.com/listing/122621679/pink-argyle-business-card-case-duck-tape?ref=exp_listing

Madge Collection: https://maxinecollection.wordpress.com/

Max & Myron Books: http://www.amazon.com/s/ref=nb_sb_noss?url=search-alias%3Dstripbooks&field-keywords=Max+and+Myron%2C+VanHatten&rh=n%3A283155%2Ck%3AMax+and+Myron\c+VanHatten

Merrium Webster, Word Games: http://www.merriam-webster.com/game/index.htm

Mr. Fred Rogers' singing Won't You Be My Neighbor: https://vimeo.com/122032164

My Facebook Cover Images— http://www.myfbcover.in/typography-facebook-covers/my-friends-rock-facebook-cover.html

National Braille Press: https://www.nbp.org/

North Texas Food Bank, Virtual Food Drive: http://web.ntfb.org/get-involved/donate-food/virtual-food-drive

Paths to Literacy, Learn Braille: http://www.pathstoliteracy.org/resources/resources-learn-braille

Pet Sitters International: https://www.petsit.com/takeyourdog/

Pun of the Day: http://www.punoftheday.com/cgi-bin/disppuns.pl?ord=S&cat=3&sub=0307&page=1

SOS Day Official Website: http://thesosday.com/

SynCardia: http://www.syncardia.com

Take Your Dog to Work Day: http://www.chiff.com/business/take-your-dog-work-day.htm

Wellcat Holidays: www.wellcat.com

Word Games: http://www.wordgames.com/

Word Game World: http://www.word-game-world.com/printable-word-games.html

Whale Times, Hagfish Activities: http://whaletimes.org/?cat=2

You Give Goods, Virtual Food Drive Setup: https://yougivegoods.com/how-it-works?gclid=CjwKEAjwho2x-BRD0mpzUvsya6SgSJAAkRepSsH8TNS1B6115bTGFNMY9TLSD02bduioFdo8o9eQR9hoCS57w_wcB

About the Author

Having been a business owner for most of her adult life, operating a multi–million dollar surgical clinic and a local barbeque take-out to list just a couple, have given Ginger Marks the insight needed to assist business owners from all walks of life.

Ginger is the owner of the Calomar, LLC which holds her DocUmeant family of companies. The various entities all work towards a common goal that just happens to be their tagline; "We Make YOU Look GOOD!" Her services include both publishing and digital design assistance. She is proud of the fact that she is able to give high quality, efficient service at a remarkably reasonable rate. It is for this reason she chose to list her publishing company in New York City while residing in Florida.

When Ginger decided to embark on a writing career it was of no surprise to her mother, who herself is a published author. Her love for the arts is what spurred her to hone her talents as a digital designer, offering services to business owners and authors alike.

DocUmeant.net offers editing and writing services; DocUmeantDesigns.com, as you would guess, focuses on designs ranging from websites to book covers & layouts to buttons and business stationary needs; while DocUmeantPublishing.com's focus was begun with the Self-published author in mind. Now with ten years of experience in publishing she has built her success in the global community.

Ginger is a member of DesignFirms where she is a top rated designer, SPANpro (Small Publishers Association of North America), IBPA (International Book Publishers Association), DBW (Digital Book World), and is on the board of FAPA as VP Communications (Florida Authors and Publishers Association).

In 2012 she was awarded VIP membership to Covington's Who's Who and her publishing company, DocUmeant Publishing, was awarded the 2012 New York Award in the Publishing Consultants & Services category by the U.S. Commerce Association (USCA). She recently won the 2015 Clearwater, FL Design Firm Award and has won book cover design awards and took home the silver medal for the *2015 Weird & Wacky Holiday Marketing Guide* from FAPA.

In her spare time she loves to do crafts of all sorts and sing. And yes, she is a little wacky at times too which keeps her fun and inspiring. Ginger lives in Florida where she works side-by-side with her husband, Philip, who is VP Editing for DocUmeant Publishing.

To contact Ginger whether for publish, design, or interviews you may reach her at ginger.marks@documeantdesigns.com or at 727-565-2130.

Notes to Self

Weird & Wacky Holiday Marketing Plan

Holiday Title:

Holiday Date:

Begin Preparation Date:

Type of Event:

List of possible Joint Venture Partners:

Media Contacted:

Comments on how it went:

Weird & Wacky Holiday Marketing Plan

Holiday Title:

Holiday Date:

Begin Preparation Date:

Type of Event:

List of possible Joint Venture Partners:

Media Contacted:

Comments on how it went:

Weird & Wacky Holiday Marketing Plan

Holiday Title:

Holiday Date:

Begin Preparation Date:

Type of Event:

List of possible Joint Venture Partners:

Media Contacted:

Comments on how it went:

Weird & Wacky Holiday Marketing Plan

Holiday Title:

Holiday Date:

Begin Preparation Date:

Type of Event:

List of possible Joint Venture Partners:

Media Contacted:

Comments on how it went:

Weird & Wacky Holiday Marketing Plan

Weird & Wacky Holiday Marketing Plan

Holiday Title:

Holiday Date:

Begin Preparation Date:

Type of Event:

List of possible Joint Venture Partners:

Media Contacted:

Comments on how it went:

Weird & Wacky Holiday Marketing Plan

Holiday Title:

Holiday Date:

Begin Preparation Date:

Type of Event:

List of possible Joint Venture Partners:

Media Contacted:

Comments on how it went:

www.ingramcontent.com/pod-product-compliance
Lightning Source LLC
Chambersburg PA
CBHW061233270326
41929CB00030B/3476